Text copyright

© 2018 Ryan Dawson

All Rights Reserved

Edited by Ryan Dawson

Cover art anonymous

All photos and illustrations contained within this book are reproduced with the permission of their respective creators.

For more books, videos and audio recordings by Ryan Dawson, or to contact the author, visit
http://www.ancreport.com

Special Thanks

Kehinde Sonola, Thread 6, ANC Patreon, YJ Moon, Ryu, Leo, J.A.
M. Rivero, Stan, Mike and Tammy, Maidch, Shaun, Tim, TS, RP,
and LCAM

My family and all the people from
http://www.ancreport.com

Without you, none of my work would be possible.

Thank you. This book was made possible by people like you,
the reader. I could not do it without you. Telling the truth is far
cheaper than lying to people. Together we can change the system.
Parts of this book may be triggering. If you are a grown up, then this
won't be a problem. If you are an idiot, or are sensitive to things like
facts, logic and records then please continue reading in a room away
from windows or fragile objects.

Democracy at its philosophical root has always relied on the
assumption of an informed and educated public. Without those
ingredients, the democratic method fails. Our current rent-a-
government system exists because the public is denied crucial
information by the entertainment-rich corporate press. Knowledge is
power, and with control of some media in our hands, the plutocrats
can no longer operate in the dark.

But we have to take action. We should be using the power of
referendum more often. It is possible at least in the US to circumvent
the paid-off congress through direct democracy like that. Referendums
can be used for much more than just legalizing marijuana. That's only
a start. We need to run for local offices. Turn off your TV when the
daily dose of corporate news comes on. Let their ratings continue to

plummet and their tune will change. Remember that we are the majority.

Most people are not psychopaths. Most people do not support pointless wars, even with all the millions of dollars spent on propaganda. Most people, around the world, oppose the NSA, the TSA, the CIA, the IMF, drone strikes, predatory lending, government waste and corporate welfare. From the Starbucks wooly-beast to the kid in a basement making Pepe Memes, there is common ground against government waste, violence, and stupidity.

We do not have to choose between the lesser of two evils. The plutocrat's power hangs on their ability to manipulate the electoral process, which in turn relies on the ability to control the mass media. That is why your support for independent media is so vital. So I thank you for all of your time and your support. Let's keep moving forward.

Thank you!

Ryan Dawson

Table of Contents

Introduction

Political discussions often get emotionally charged, with some of the participants clinging to titles like a fan boy to his favorite sports team. Part of what contributes to this is the vague terminology involved in politics, which can be confusing. It's important not to get hung up on such subjective terms, focusing instead more on the content than the labels. Many terms vary from place to place, or era to era.

In Japan and some parts of Europe, for example, the term "liberal" actually carries the same meaning as "conservative" does in the United States. Japan's ruling Liberal Democratic Party is anything but liberal, at least by US standards. Even within a given state, political terms change or flip their meaning over time.

For many years the Republican Party in the US was associated with the conservative movement and was seen as the champion of fiscal responsibility. Over time, however, its core aims have moved towards evangelical social values. The word liberal (with a small "L") means someone accepting and lenient. However, as a political alignment Liberal (with a big "L"), it is only socially open within a narrow parameter and economically restrictive. Increasingly, this is drifting towards pretentious safe moral crusades against "isms" real or imagined. If this trend persist, we could see a division in the left between those concerned with a classic Liberal core value like labor and those on a directionless social justice crusade, which seems to be mostly about the participants feelings than any particular policiy.

Some people are shocked to learn that, in the US, the Democratic Party that now associates itself with Liberals was the same party responsible for starting World War I, World War II, the Korean War, and the Vietnam War, not to mention the invasion of Libya, the continued wars in Afghanistan and Iraq, the proxy war in Syria, and today's ever-increasing drone strikes in Pakistan and Yemen. For those people for whom history started in the year 2000 with George Bush as President, the Republicans are the war party, even though the balance of history proves them to have been the war opposition party.

This phase shift has prompted many to call the members of the current Republican (or Conservative) Party the neo-conservatives, or "neocons". They have become a combination of the old 1980s, Cold-War Republicans, which based their core around hating Communism, and religious partisans with distinctly pro-Israeli loyalties.

Across the pond in the UK, a similar ideological group has sprung up inside the Liberal Party, the British counterpart to our Republicans. Its members, appropriately referred to as "neo-liberals", are composed of hardline interventionists and big- government supporters, which prefer foreign warfare to domestic welfare. They are a combination of what may be the worst aspects of the previous left-right paradigm: socially conservative and fiscally liberal.

But when you really look at the evolution of political parties through history, you can see that it is usually only the labels which change over time; the underlying constant is that the pro-war, pro-big government party typically ends up being whichever one happens to be in charge at the time. The supporters who voted them in might see it differently, but policy makers, regardless of label, tend to follow the beat of the same drummer.

The progressive label, too, has its own problems. While it sounds like a movement that should idealize progress, the progressive ideology is an extreme, leftist position that tends to favor the expansion of the nanny state. It was the empowerment of the nanny state which led to American Prohibition in the 1920s, which was the legalization of a social ban that was ironically more in line with the views of the religious right than the socially liberal left.

Since abandoning all talk about supporting labor, the only real activity the left continues to engage in is a frantic, often theatrical, expression of who among them is the most anti-racist or anti-sexist. The simple act of not being racist/sexist is really not something worth patting oneself on the back about, as in any normal society it should be considered, well, normal. Giving yourself credit for not being racist is like congratulating yourself on not beating your kids.

The base of the right, on the other hand, seems to be split into two interests: how openly they can wear Jesus on their sleeve, or how loudly they can express their utter disdain for welfare, which they believe only serves to encourage laziness and freeloading, with extra points if it is done by illegals. Political discourse with either of these camps rarely advances beyond these two subjects.

A general view holds that the left supports bigger government and the right smaller. Not true. The right may claim to support less government intervention in the marketplace, but they are more likely to interfere in social issues like the legalization of drugs, abortion or homosexual marriage. Likewise the left may be more open on certain social issues, but more restrictive on business (i.e. entrepreneurs).

In addition to this, much of their well intended do-gooder intervention on behalf of social equality, such as affirmative action, welfare and guaranteed student loans, makes things worse. Even worse are the campaigns of so-called humanitarian military intervention, when America goes to war in the name of liberating ethnic minorities, upholding women's rights, and (the most insane one) preventing slaughter by slaughtering someone else first, such as was done to Libya. All of these often backfire and only serve to exacerbate the very problems they claim to be trying to solve.

On a macro level, both major political parties in the US are exactly the same. They hold to the same monetary policies, the same foreign policies (albeit with different spin), and the same systems of corporate welfare and foreign aid. They give free rein to the CIA, rationalize torture, and encourage domestic spying. They support massive deficit spending and putting in place international trade agreements like NAFTA and TPP that supersede the democratic process. They spend billions on the war on drugs, the war on terror, blind support for Israel and the corporate lobbies, and on bailouts for financial institutions "too big to fail".

The only differences between them are how they demographically brand themselves, some slight variations on tax policies, and the amount of hot air they manage to expel about the relatively insignificant wedge issues.

If a person were to take a blind test, in which they were challenged to correctly attribute which political policies belonged to George W. Bush versus Barack Obama, they'd be hard pressed to tell the difference. Both were pro-war, pro-torture, favored corporate bailouts and domestic spying, and supported the expansion of NATO and the continuance of the Patriot Act.

That is why I strongly encourage you, the reader, to look past the arbitrary labels of the left-right paradigm and tribalist loyalties to a particular party. When it comes to the mismanagement of the major financial and political issues which affect our daily lives, they are both to blame.

This book is not about cheerleading for a specific team. It's about showing the effects on our country that have been brought about by the dangerous fusion of business and state. It doesn't matter if you view the problem as the state enriching itself through favoritism towards certain corporations, or conversely one of corporations bribing the state to gain control of members of government or lucrative investment deals. It's all the same result. It doesn't matter if you see the snake from head to tail, or from tail to head; it's still the same snake.

Government and banking institutions, at least in their current incarnation, exist primarily to ensure the transfer wealth from you to themselves, hiding behind the promise of providing you with particular services to benefit the public good.

The truth is, as matters stand now they are taking far more than they are giving. The government now serves primarily as the enforcement arm of the corporate class, which through its power of force and law, maintains the status of the plutocracy.

The recent banker bailouts were a financial scandal which managed to move around not just trillions, but tens of trillions of dollars in public funds, earning the dubious privilege of being the largest financial scandal in human history. Our (USA) national debt as it stands now is un-payable; the trillions spent annually on needless wars of choice and disastrous covert operations only serve to increase that debt and ensure the reciprocal hostility of the rest of the world. If we do not act to break the poisonous relationship that exists between corporation and state, it is we the people who will break.

The 2008 housing bubble bailouts were the largest financial scandal in History. Tens of trillions of dollars were needed to prop up institutions which had engaged in fraud. This wasn't the result of a lack of regulations. This was the result of criminal behavior. Investment banks illegally bribed rating agencies, so they could offload toxic securities onto third parties. Private profits and public debt could not work without the marriage between business and state. But it is not just in banking where the reverse Midas touch of government rears its rotten finger. Everything from healthcare, to education to the military to even the mail is made more expensive and dysfunctional by "government help." Making matters worse, is how the cult of political correctness and SJW outrage culture, turns every issue into a race/sex/prejudice issue. This, "agree with us or you're a Nazi," bully tactic has in a great degree silenced many reasonable solutions and ideas.

Well trigger warning. If facts offend you, then blame your own ignorance. Grownups need to talk about serious issues without the victimhood pissing contest overtaking the narrative.

CHAPTER 1

State vs. Corporation: The Blame Game

"The Right's view of big government and the Left's view of big business are both correct." -Robert Anton Wilson

Politics and economics affect you whether you choose to engage in them or not. Ignorance is not bliss. Not knowing a giant spike in gas is coming or that writing the wrong thing on social media years ago could get your account banned or even get you jailed in some totalitarian places like the UK isn't good. Everyone's life must respond to political and economic issues no matter how little attention the individual chooses to pay them. This book is US centric, but examples of state failings can be shown to scale anywhere.

It is odd that the subject of politics is categorically considered taboo never to be discussed in polite company. Some economic theories likewise inspire a level of dogmatic loyalty that would put the most passionate religious fanatic to shame. All in all, this makes these critical matters very hard to talk about. Without discourse there can be no improvements, which in turn makes it very difficult to change things in a constructive fashion.

And the group that really benefits from such taboos? Not a special interest or a diabolical conspiracy; merely the status quo. The well-intentioned dislike of offending others has created a climate that inhibits the questioning of authority, regardless of its level of abuse.

Government corruption and stupidity is just accepted with a shrug as something inevitable. It's just the way things are and can't be changed, so why even talk about it?

That's not to say you can't have some kind of discussion at all, but even if you manage to do so it will be only within very narrow parameters.

There are many problems in our political system, not to mention how it's covered by the media, and the changes we need cannot be initiated as long as there remains a social stigma attached to talking politics.

What little is offered by the mass media on the subject is by and large useless garbage. The powerfully demarcated left-right paradigm, the labels used to explain certain economic models, the demographic associations with political parties – they are all forms of obfuscation. Economic and political discourses are riddled with false dichotomies, and political history itself is saturated with twisted propaganda and outright lies.

Political reporting on television has sunk to such a low quality that we now accept television pundits like Chris Matthews who say "agree with me or you're a racist!", or Bill O'Reilly shouting down his guests and screaming profanities at his co-workers. We have lobbyists given carte blanche to write bills for a congress who passes them without even bothering to read them first. Multi-billion dollar institutions use our government to implement a collective policy of Robin Hood in reverse.

The US president, the leader of the free world, now has a kill list that includes the names of American citizens. The new security state being implemented all over the globe, has airports taking nude pictures of passengers in the name of fighting terrorism. The NSA taps the communications of every citizen without the need for permission or justification. And to top it all off, the US government spends trillions in its pursuit of death through war.

In addition, our government gave $10.5 billion in bailouts to General Motors, a corporation that helped Detroit earn the nickname "Motor City", and yet can't find the $3.5 billion necessary to help save the city itself from bankruptcy. Yet $3.5 billion is the kind of sum the US will give to a foreign state every year. So while Congress can find enough spare change in the couch cushions to not only save a major corporation from its own bad business practices and go on to subsidize Israel's ethnic cleansing, they can't seem figure out how to pay for the pensions of hard- working Americans in Detroit. Death and corruption get funding; life doesn't. That is not to say that government spending is a solution for Detroit either. If not for crooked unions and wealth distribution from the productive to the state connected, there wouldn't be a pension problem. If property taxes were not hiked beyond the real value of the homes there wouldn't be so many abandoned unsellable properties.

America desperately needs a separation between business and state. There is such a system, which already has a name (now intentionally polluted by some), known as free-market capitalism. We as a nation need to return to a form of capitalism that is untainted by rampant, state-sponsored favoritism for only those select businesses with ties to members of the government. It's time for "we the people" to take a long, measured look at the economics and politics that drive our nation, minus all the agenda-driven spin.

Even when it comes to the modern take on capitalism there exist two polarized views. There are those who think the invisible hand of the Free Market will take care of everything, and all economic injustices and problems stem from government intervention. Then there are those who paint capitalism as the greatest evil in history, responsible for every modern war, the blight of wage slavery, the return to sweatshop labor and an ever-increasing wealth disparity. They believe that capitalism has nothing whatsoever to do with ensuring individual liberty or economic mobility, and that the government is naturally benevolent; it's the corporations who are destroying everything.

Neither faction will step out of their own sound chamber long enough to acknowledge the reality that, given enough opportunity and motivation, corporations will bribe the government. Government officials are just people themselves, and as such perhaps even more likely to use government to enrich themselves than to serve the public interest. The greatest evil is when these two forces collaborate to work together. When this happens, you get a form of fascism. This is not to evoke the image of the old cliché of people goose-stepping in the street. However, a country can be fascist without all the costumes and theatrics.

No matter the extremeness of their position, each side of this argument makes valid criticisms about the current relationship between the government and corporations. The balance of these opposing views cannot be construed to say that the truth lies precisely in the middle, either. It would be dismissive to label all critics of capitalism as communist; just as it would be to label critics of government intervention as individuals beholden to the corporate fat cats, or as dog-eat-dog anarchists. Just as the majority of libertarians are certainly not fat cats, the majority of progressives are by no means communist or socialist.

Regardless, the majority of the economic woes currently plaguing the United States can be clearly tied to the government. It is due to the government's increasing willingness to intervene in the marketplace that the lucrative "rent-a-government" bribery system has come into being. The main reason corporations now regularly spend millions of dollars a year on lobbying is because it makes the most business sense; every dollar they spend results in a much larger return.

All the regulation in the world isn't going to matter when it's being written by big businesses and government employees who are in bed with each other. The common issue is that it is the state which acts as the facilitator in these relationships. An appropriate analogy would be to say that it's more effective to go after the guy giving away the free alcohol than it is to chase down all the alcoholics. Without the power of force from the government, corporations could not do to scale all the injustices they currently can do without consequence. Think of the government as the military wing of a massive corporate conglomerate. Separate it from the rest and resolution can then begin

The worst part of all of this is that, in order to fund all of its various schemes and partnerships, the state uses the collateral of our tax dollars to borrow money from the central banks. In the end, the politicians, the businesses and their lobbyists are all perfectly content to leave the ultimate burden of repayment on the backs of the taxpayers. This begets a system where people can give away other people's money in order to enrich themselves and their friends.

Even when their intentions are good (a rare condition in government), policy-makers can still screw things up through sheer incompetence or a pronounced lack of foresight. If we took away the power of the state to pick winners and losers in the marketplace, crony capitalists would not have a cash cow to award themselves monopolies, bailouts, or be able to stifle their competition through their self-tailored regulations. The real reason capitalism is getting a bad name is because we refuse to actually practice it.

Some people blame not enough government regulation and inadequate taxes on the wealthy for the social and economic woes of the nation. For instance, they will point to the repeal of the Glass-Steagall Act, which restricted affiliations between investment banks and securities firms, as the main contributing factor to the 2008 financial disaster.

Indeed, such a rare good regulation might be seen as an example of the government reducing the power of banks. Even before it was repealed, however, regulators had already all but killed it by issuing new interpretations of the act that were upheld by courts, and which permitted banks and their affiliates to engage in an increasing variety of securities-related activities. By the time of the final repeal in 1999, the system had already deviated so far that it made little real impact.

One good regulation does not mean that regulations in general are the way to prosperity. Likewise, one bad regulation does not mean that any regulation at all will be the doom of American business. They must be evaluated on a case-by-case basis.

Still, it seems that for every good regulation, there are a multitude of bad ones. The reason that good ones are so rare is because the government's greed often exceeds its benevolence. People must recognize that the state has no incentive to use its regulatory powers for any purpose other than to enrich itself and its corporate partners. The examples are endless. There is no reason for the state to redistribute tax money from anyone, rich or not, to help the needy, when it can just as easily waste the money on more wars and bailouts from which government officials directly profit.

There is never a political consequence for this kind behavior. Incumbents enjoy reelection rates above 90%, regardless of what they have done (short of a disastrous scandal). And it is they who make the laws not the president.

One of the great mistakes Liberals and progressives make is the tendency to judge policies and programs by their intentions rather than their results. The good intentions allows for virtue signaling and psychological gratification. It is because of this that it is very hard to change policies that are not working without being chastised and labeled a bad person who doesn't agree with their intentions.

Libertarians and progressives agree that America is immersed in corporatism. While progressives may see Libertarians as cold-hearted, and Libertarians see progressives as detached from reality, they share a mutual desire to end corporatism. But progressives are in love with what sounds good rather than what is good.

Raising the minimum wage, sounds good, it sounds like you are increasing the income of the lowest earners. Opposing a wage raise sounds bad. It sounds like you are in favor of exploitation. The same can be said for rent control, price controls on goods, and other lofty sounding ideas which appear to champion the poor. The real world results however are different.

Price controls cause shortages, of housing, of food or whatever is underpriced and in the long run this hurts the entire public not just the poor. Raising wages can price many people right out of a job. It also reduces start up businesses which in turn gives established businesses less competition and more of a monopoly. A person has to produce more than what they are being paid otherwise there is no reason to hire them at all.

Getting rid of tipping does not mean one hates the person who has to take tips. Lots of countries don't tip and have great service. However the resistance to change is stemming from an emotional sense of self righteousness where by one, who is usually not directly affected, can lobby on behalf of a group and feel like a good person. Poor results from programs decades old do little to sway the minds of the self righteous. In fact, merely disagreeing with them, will in their minds, mean that you are against the poor, women, minorities, the youth, or whatever medium is being used to fuel their sense of moral superiority. It is wrong to approach such people with arguments of logic and reason. An asymmetric psychological approach works better. Comedy and group think is one powerful method. This way they can still feel smug and superior yet be directed to abandon bad policies. It is amazing the amount of damage a South Park or Family Guy can do to a Yelp or Whole Foods culture, through satire.

The government may be corrupt, but the market is neutral. We may long for something better, but that kind of political change is not going to happen without social and intellectual changes. Our focus must not be placed solely on the government or the corporations; a finger-pointing contest as to which is worse is hardly constructive.

A third set of players, which do not fall neatly within the realm of government or business, are the banks. They do not sell goods; their only commodity is money. This is very different from any other kind of business. In the United States, the central bank controls the nation's money supply. The quantity of available money may be the most important factor in determining the American quality of life. This is where we must begin

CHAPTER 2

Banking Corruption

"I believe that banking institutions are more dangerous to our liberties than standing armies."

– Thomas Jefferson

The US government is not the only entity responsible for disposing of the nation's funds; this power is also held by the Federal Reserve. Contrary to popular belief, the Federal Reserve, often referred to simply as "the Fed", is not part of the actual government. It is a private banking system, although not in the normal sense, as the government has granted it extraordinary powers that would never be afforded to an ordinary institution. As Thomas DiLorenzo pointed out, "[The Fed is] the biggest and most important **regulatory capture** of all …

The Fed was created as a governmental cartel enforcement mechanism for the banking industry."[1]

The creation of what would become the Fed was carried out in secret on Jekyll Island by Senator Nelson Aldrich and a cabal of prominent bankers, as was noted by Eustace Mullins in his book, The Secrets of the Federal Reserve. He wrote, "The [Senator Nelsen] Aldrich group journeyed [to Jekyll Island] as the place to draft the plan for control of the money and credit of the people of the United States."[2]

Officially, the government created the Fed with the Federal Reserve

Act of 1913. Although it is not part of the government, it owes its existence and the powers it was granted to the government, and the president plays a role in appointing its chairman. It sets the interest rates of the market, thus preempting the ability of the market to set them on its own. This is not to say that the government should not play a role in the nation's currency; on the contrary, The US Constitution states that it is the job of Congress to create and maintain the money supply in the name of the public good.

It does not, however, grant special powers to a private bank to lend out and collect interest on it for its own gain.

This is (or at least should be) common sense. Monetary policy ought to be the center of political discussions within the legislative branch, since everything that involves money stems from it. And yet it's never treated as a primary issue; it's not even a secondary issue.

There have been candidates for the presidency, such as William Jennings Bryan and Dr. Ron Paul, who have attempted to bring awareness to the issues surrounding monetary policy, and to the idiocy that is the Federal Reserve System. But the bankers, with the full might of the mass media to back them up, came down on them as hard as they could. Despite multiple attempts, neither of these men was able to win the presidency.

Before the creation of the central banks there were also no world wars, as it would have been impossible to finance them. Banks now possess the power to drive entire nations into debt without firing a single bullet. They can devastate a country through predatory lending, in which they target not individual corporations, but the government itself. This works because a government doesn't actually spend its own money. That is to say, the individuals which make up a government get paid for what they do regardless of the debt they help create through their work within the government.

It is because of this contradiction that banks can affect an entire government by bribing a few key people and thus create situation where the government as a whole is willing to sell its own country down the river. And this is exactly what the IMF and World Bank routinely do while working in tandem with various intelligence agencies. The physical location of a bank hardly matters, either; it will assault its own countrymen just as quickly as anyone else if there's a profit to be made.

Because of the relationship between banks and the state, we have created the largest nanny state of all: a nanny state for the corporations. Financial institutions can now swindle whomever they want without any risk to themselves. This happened in 2008 with the popping of the housing bubble.

The federal government's solution was to work with the Federal Reserve and create a massive bailout to protect the financial gamblers responsible for the disaster.

Many libertarians and progressives strongly opposed the bailouts. The libertarians did on philosophical principle: bailouts create a moral hazard for businesses. They represent the state intervening in the market and rewarding the failure of companies that should otherwise go bankrupt.

Progressives opposed the bailouts because they oppose what they see as an unethical system designed to help the rich get richer. As taxing the rich to balance the distribution of wealth is central to the American progressive ideology, awarding the wealthy for their mistakes with even more wealth is an abhorrent concept. Regardless of the differences in their ideological motivation, at least on this there was some unity between libertarians and progressives: bailouts are bad.

Now the corporate welfare junkies at this time were defending themselves with the nonsensical slogan, "too big to fail". Progressives placed the blame for the bubble on capitalism out of control, desperately in need of more government oversight. They maintained that the bailouts stemmed from a culture of corporate bribery and a lack of regulation in the marketplace. By this logic it would seem that even when it is the government spending the money, it is still the private sector's fault for taking it.

Yet once the government starts controlling market capital in the market, it is by definition no longer a free market. Take away the government's power to award corporations money and you won't have them clamoring for their piece of it anymore. Knowing what the inevitable outcome would be, would the financial institutions have behaved the way they did if they hadn't already foreseen the government ensuring that they could not fail? Probably not.

Despite the deep flaws of the system as it stands now, had we let the banks who had gambled with our lives and our money just fail as they deserved, they would have brought a lot of innocent people down with them. The market correction would still have been painful, and not just for the banks, but for much of the nation. However, it would not have been nearly as bad or as long of a depression as that which corporate welfare has created. The Fed can cause a crash in what it calls the business cycle simply by calling in its loans, which then causes a reduction in the physical money supply.

This has a direct impact on American unemployment. Despite the demand for skilled labor and the availability of people with the necessary skills, there simply isn't enough money available to pay them. The quantity of money available is essential. When two-thirds of the money supply is tied up in endless speculation (a polite word for gambling), everyone actually working and creating product for money suffers. When the speculation is being done with credit instead of capital, we all suffer in the end.

Credit bubbles have an adverse impact on the stock market, as a large portion of the stock investments are made using borrowed money that does not even actually exist in the current money supply.

While there is no utopian model to solve all problems there certainly is a better and a worse. The free market allows for corrections after the fact, but failure is absolutely essential for success. If you won't allow failure then you foster irresponsibility and make every problem longer, more damaging, and harder to recover from.

While the bursting of the housing bubble was blamed by some political factions on the follies of unregulated capitalism, prominent supporters of the free market had long predicted its collapse. Not only did they predict it, they also explained with great accuracy how and why it was going to fail. Few listened; the media ridiculed them and labeled them as "crazies", although it was the crazies who would be proven right in the end. The housing bubble was anything but capitalism.

Too many people with too many big houses is a problem other economic systems such as communism or socialism would love to have. People caught up in the collapse lost things they never would have been able to obtain in the first place under other economic systems. The housing bubble was a pyramid of escalating IOUs created erroneously out of horrible credit. Credit is by definition not capital, and yet its excessive granting was encouraged by a climate of extreme moral hazard.

Noted documentarian Bill Still summed up the problem wonderfully: "The truth is governments generally aren't printing money wildly, governments are borrowing money wildly."[3] This is an unfortunate fact of modern economics. What gain is there in paying interest, an extra unnecessary layer for money, when the same amount of money can be created interest-free?

The biggest check to prevent irresponsibility on the part of the lender issuing the loans is the risk of default. If the receiver defaults, the lender cannot not get their money back.

Even though a bank can seize assets, the assets cannot be quickly liquidated, and so the lender must take on a risk with each loan they make. This natural degree of risk was removed by changing how loans were issued and separating the responsibility of collecting payments away from the party creating the loans. Compounding that problem was not simply a lack of oversight or regulatory requirements to limit the fractional reserve ratio for the lending institutions. (The fractional reserve ratio is how much a bank can loan out relative to how much money it actually holds from deposits.)

Banks always loan out more than they actually have, as the odds that everyone will come and withdraw their money on the same day are close to zero. The bank counts on this tendency to create wealth for itself by collecting the loan amount back plus interest.

For example, if 20 people each give a bank fifty dollars it will have a thousand dollars in physical cash If the fractional reserve ratio is set at 3 to 1, that means the bank can loan out up to $3,000 in credit. So long as most of the loans are repaid on schedule, the bank can cover its deposits while making real money off of the fictitious money handed out in the loan. Obviously, the larger the ratio becomes and the fewer people keep up on their loan payments, the greater risk there is of a potential disaster.

Every bank in the world practices this system of fractional reserve lending. What happened in America during the financial crisis was caused by a much deeper, systemic problem, not merely a miscalculation or screw-up. It was, in fact, a completely criminal, calculated strategy.

Corporate greed and the government that enables it have created the financial crisis we have today. To punish either side of this equation to the exclusion of the other would be foolish, and there is no justification to simply pick a side and defend it like a favorite sports team. Regulation (or the absence thereof) is not an inherently evil thing. Whether a regulation is good or bad depends on what it does, and some regulation can be beneficial. When it's not is when the government uses regulation in order to protect its mercantilist partners in crime, rather than the public.

A truly free market already has natural regulations of its own built in, such as the possibility of failure. In fact, you could say the government is serving to deregulate the market by intervening with these natural checks and balances. When it comes to the concepts of regulation or deregulation, categorically rejecting or accepting the use of either strategy will only lead to trouble.

Be careful of false dichotomies in politics. It is a bizarre phenomenon, but even the most intelligent people can get pulled into brand-like, extremist

Political dogma. Likewise, some think that the definition of open-mindedness means the complete acceptance or rejection of all established theories. In reality, that could be described as a state of being "no-minded". One must learn to think critically in order to solve problems on a case-by-case basis. There are no simple formulas or shortcuts.

CHAPTER 3

The Housing Bubble

"It is well enough that people of the nation do not understand our banking and monetary system, for if they did, I believe there would be a

revolution before tomorrow morning."

– Henry Ford

In order to analyze what led to the housing bubble and the subsequent crash of 2008, let's compare the old and new systems of creating and paying for a mortgage. In the old system, the home buyer would deal directly with the lender. The lender incurred a risk by creating a mortgage, because the system assumed it would take twenty to thirty years before the home buyer could pay it off completely.

The potential home buyer then had to provide documentation of his income and credit rating to the lender in order to prove they could make their mortgage payments every month. In addition, a down payment was also usually required, an accepted practice that was considered completely normal.

Once the mortgage was granted, the monthly payments were paid to the bank, which made money off of them by collecting interest over the period of the loan.

This system, however, was often subject to usury, a practice whereby a bank makes more money than can be justified by the services it provides. Simply put, the bank makes money using someone else's work to provide a loan using someone else's money. In theory the bank's job in granting a loan is to provide coordination and management; it gathers money from deposits made by one person or several, and gives that sum to the loan recipient. The bank then charges interest, which is justified by its use to pay the employees of the bank.

Most of the time, though, the money the bank loans out doesn't come from actual deposits. The banks have perfected a system that allows them to loan out money they do not physically possess and then, through the loan payments, to collect the virtual money they created, plus interest. They have become a third-party middleman that does almost nothing beyond collecting money, loaning it out, and then collecting more money from that in the form of interest.

That such entities exist seems unfair enough. That is not to say that banking itself is unnecessary. Just like any system, when it functions well, it can actually be quite beneficial for society. But the new system which caused the 2008 housing bubble was far worse, and much more dangerous.

In the new system, the lending institutions sold the mortgages they made with home buyers to investment banks. What they sold them was a new type of number-juggling I like to call a "TOU" (They Owe You). It didn't matter if the home buyer could pay back their loan or not, because once the lender sold the mortgage off to the investment bank, they no longer bore the risk of people defaulting on their payments. Thus the lenders had a huge incentive to loan to lots of people, since they weren't incurring any risk to themselves.

So they started making loans to a new group of people they called "subprime candidates" – an impressive-sounding label that served the ironic purpose of glossing over just how far below prime these people were ("toxic" would have been a more accurate description). Sometimes these were people who were already in debt, had no collateral at all and were not even required to provide documentation of their credit history or financial standing. They were then given massive loans, which the lending institutions knew in advance they could not repay. Instead, they passed the burden of collection on to the investment banks.

To exacerbate the problem, the Federal Reserve decided to lower interest rates, thus leading to the lending institutions lowering their own rates in order to encourage more borrowing. And it worked. People believed they had to seize the opportunity to borrow while the interest rates were so low.

People borrowed not only for homes but also for businesses, all the while believing, "Wow! I have to do it now. Everyone else is!" Then came countless TV shows showing people how they could flip a house on their own (essentially, "flipping" refers to a hands-on investment technique where someone buys a house on credit, fixes it up himself and then sells it for more than the original amount owed). Still other enterprising individuals would buy a house, live in it for a couple of years as a method to avoid capital gains tax, and then sell it again for more than the original loan. These strategies shared a common, fundamental flaw, which is that there must eventually be a last person left to hold the bag.

As a result, houses became commodities, a mere thing to be traded, rather than homes where people live. A house became thought of as an asset one could use to gamble with and get rich quick. But the purchases of such were being made, not with capital, but with credit – and very bad credit at that. Rather than using actual currency, home buyers were now using loan number two to pay for loan number one. That is what is also now commonly known as a Ponzi scheme, and it is always destined to fail.

People who could not afford homes bought them anyway, in part because the media was manipulating them. Many families were also suckered in by so- called teaser rates. That is to say they received a low- interest, adjustable-rate mortgage (ARM), which then at the end of a two-year period would shoot up dramatically. The only way out for a family who could never really afford it in the first place was to sell the house and pass the problem on to someone else, who would most likely be in the same predicament. This influx of generous credit to essentially anyone regardless of means greatly inflated housing cost of housing.

While the banks were busy luring their irresponsible, "subprime" borrowers into disastrous debt, the credit bubble was forcing responsible, hard-working people with actual savings and no debt out of the chance of home ownership. As a result they found themselves with few options on where to live because of the skyrocketing housing prices. They would either be forced to pay too much for a home, or couldn't even find one in the first place.

These were people trying to start a new family, or perhaps just finishing college and going to work in a new city, and thus were in need of a new place to live These folks wanted a home because that is where they were planning to live. They weren't buying a home to try to flip it or sell it later to someone else; they intended to make a life in it.

And while one would think home prices should have come down as a result of the bubble bursting, they didn't. They were instead artificially supported to soften the political impact of what would otherwise have resulted in a dramatic drop in the value of homes. Since the numbers were now based on credit rather than capital, the properties were greatly over- appraised.

These too-high valuations didn't drop, either, as they continued to be based upon the previous, faulty ratings. The truth is the only solution would be to simply liquidate all of these bad assets. But the bubble was not simply the fault of aspiring speculators or prospective homeowners trying to live beyond their mean; there are always at least two parties in any loan.

So the question remains: why would the investment banks buy a bunch of risky loans? The investment banks had their own scheme. Five principle investment banks really threw gas on the fire: Goldman Sachs, Morgan Stanley, Lehman Brothers, Merrill Lynch, and Bear Stearns. They bought bogus securities from the lending banks and packaged the subprime loans into something called complex derivatives or CDOs (collateralized debt obligations)[4]

Since they didn't actually have collateral and simply ignored their obligations, one could see this as a very entertaining misnomer.

To make a CDO, the investment banks took a bunch of bad, medium, and outright horrible loans and bundled them together. One can imagine it a bit like carrying a roll of one dollar bills with a twenty on the top in order to make it look like a roll of twenties. They then took these bundled mortgages and sold them to investors through a means of deception, which involved going to the rating agencies and paying them to give these CDOs the highest, AAA ratings (this all despite the reality that they were just randomly lumped-together packages of high-risk, subprime loans).

Despite knowing that these loans were nothing more than ticking time bombs, rating agencies (including such distinguished names as Moody's, S&P, and Fitch) handed out AAA ratings[1] like candy on Halloween. The investment banks paid the rating agencies for lies

---

[1] An AAA, or triple-A rating, is the same rating given to government bonds, which are ensured by the collateral of the taxes on the population a government controls.

and then turned around and sold their junk loans to their own investors, which included a great number of European banks, not to mention normal people trying to invest their retirement funds, pension money, etc. They naturally assumed that AAA ratings guaranteed that their investments were safe, unaware that they were actually buying toxic IOUs. And did they get bailed out? No.

The best part is that the rating agencies had absolutely no liability in this scam. They were not held accountable. Of course they could claim that, technically, they hadn't lied; that they had made mistakes because of an unknown someone-or-other's gross incompetence. They dared to make such claims while getting paid by the investment banks and making jokes about just how badly they had screwed people in their emails to one another.

They were confident that they had enough plausible deniability to claim they were not being deceptive, but were in fact just really bad at their jobs (which, happily for them, is not illegal). Make no mistake, though: this was most certainly fraud. You cannot give a perfect rating to a package of sub-prime mortgages given to people with no collateral and who can't even begin to pay the principle on their loans.

How could they look at folks with such terrible credit ratings, with no or very low incomes, and say with a straight face that the loans they were awarded were as good as a government bond? The fact is that the rating agencies lied and weaseled their way out of court by claiming that the ratings that they had granted were just "their opinions", and based on such infallible testimony, got away with it. Those involved congratulated themselves on the success of such a wonderful scam, all the while bragging about the "crap they had just sold to suckers" (that's not precisely what they said, but the original version isn't fit for printing).

To make matters worse, the investment bankers, right after managing to sell their junk loans to investors by bribing the rating agencies, went around and placed bets against the very same securities they had just sold. And the scam didn't end there. After selling the CDOs to investors, the investment bank then had no risk or incentive not to go buy up more subprime loans from the lending institutions which continued to fuel this predatory lending scheme.

So the lenders were out there making as many subprime mortgages as they could find. The investment banks were gobbling them up and compiling them into as many CDOs as they could. They subsequently sold them to investors with a false rating, and then increased their revenue by betting against their own over-rated complex derivatives.

But what about leveraging?[5] Isn't that supposed to slow down such a scheme? Well it would, but rather than the normal 3-to-1 fractional reserve ratio (already bad enough), the SEC allowed the investment banks to leverage their CDOs at 33 to 1, a ratio so high as to be practically meaningless. If the CDOs' value dropped by even 2% or 3%, the lenders could go in the hole and might even bring the whole system down with them. But it didn't matter to them; this was a conspiracy, one in which they worked with the knowledge that the government would bail them out if things went wrong.

It didn't matter even if the investment bank itself went under, as the individual agents responsible were guaranteed to realize their own personal profits, measured in hundreds of millions of dollars, in the form of their own salaries as CEO, director, or management (a lot like how congressmen continue to profit at the expense of the American people). And luckily for them, the investment banks didn't go under; as a result, the criminals not only got increased bonuses but also got to keep the company.

The aforementioned ratings agencies (Standard & Poor, Moody's, and Fitch) were also not held accountable. No one went to jail. It wasn't like the savings and loans scandal of the 80's, where people actually got arrested and were put in prison. Nothing happened to those accountable at all; they just walked away with more money. They were free to gamble because it was a win/win scenario; if they won they won and if they lost, they still won.

So forget leverage; there should still be the safety valve of the insurance companies, right? Well, while they should have been, even insurance had its own scheme. AIG was the biggest culprit in this, but neither AMBAC nor MBIA were really acting as insurance companies in all of this, because rather than having actual insurance policies, where some form of collateral or portion of the monetary worth of the policy would have been available, they instead had credit default swaps.

This might seem like a confusing term, but here is how it works: first, let's look at normal insurance. Let's say you buy a house and then you buy insurance for that house. That makes for exactly one asset and one person who has insurance on it; pretty simple. An insurance company itself might buy its own risk- mitigating insurance from another insurer, itself known as a reinsurance company.

In the credit default swap system, however, a multitude of people can all get insurance on the same asset. So in essence you have multiple people betting on a single property, and if something happens to that property (if it burns down, for instance), or, as in the case of the mortgage bubble the buyer simply defaults then everyone listed as a beneficiary on the policy is going to collect.

This means that the insurance company holding the policy for all of these speculators is required to pay out to multiple parties for just one property, which is a massive burden on said company. Why a speculator might choose to gamble on insurance or place bets on whether or not someone will make their mortgage payments is beyond reasonable conjecture. This wasn't like just buying a stock, where the investment helps a corporation to create something of practical value; this was just straight-up gambling. Incidentally credit default swaps also avoided existing state regulations on insurance by using SIVs (structure investment vehicles)[6] to get around them.

In plain English this refers to a fund, usually offshore, which an investment bank creates to hide its official financial obligations. For example, if an investment bank issues a hundred million dollars' worth of mortgages to homeowners, it may then create a hundred million dollars' worth of IOUs and sell them to a SIV (IOUs on mortgages are called mortgage- backed securities). The SIV buys the mortgage-backed securities with cash and, because they count as a separate company, the obligation on the debt is not recorded on the balance sheet of the parent investment bank.

Here's the major problem, though: in order to buy the bonds (the IOUs), the SIV simply sells its own bonds by issuing commercial paper: a promissory note that has to be repaid quickly after a set number of days; usually no more than nine months at maximum. They normally carry high interest rates and can only be created by corporations with excellent credit ratings, such as Citigroup, the inventor of SIVs, and the single largest beneficiary of the bailout from the Federal Reserve. Citigroup, along with Bank of America, was also the most deeply involved in the predatory lending scheme.

To simplify the concept of the SIV, imagine if Alex borrows money from Bob and loans it to Carl. If Alex can charge Carl more interest than Bob is charging Alex, then Alex will make money in the spread between the interest rates. But what if Bob was lending money to Alex that he had gotten from Danny, who had originally borrowed it from Emily, and so on? You can see that as the chain gets longer it also becomes more dangerous as the interest at the far end increases, thus increasing the potential ridiculousness of the eventual outcome if Carl cannot pay.

It might be possible to construct a credit default swap in such a way that it was beneficial, but why roll the dice on something so convoluted and high risk? Why not just have regular insurance? Even better, allow free market insurance, which allows competition and other market forces to lower the cost naturally. Instead we have the current environment of oligopolies and unnecessary speculation.

Another benefits of the free market is that, if you fail you fail, and if you succeed, you truly succeed. It's the best form of regulation there is. Convoluted Ponzi schemes such as the subprime loan scheme merely run the risk of widespread bankruptcy. Government energies would be better spent enforcing contract law and protecting private individuals from fraud. What the United States government did was exactly the opposite of what a government should do; it protected the fraudsters and forced innocent parties not involved to foot the bill to save them.

Meanwhile, the Federal Reserve, which had set the low interest rates that helped get the fiasco started, later jacked the rate up by a factor of 17. When that became a crisis of their own making, it opened the discount window [7] to regional banks which served to do nothing but put a Band-Aid on the crack in the dam. Eventually its own greed and hubris took down the system. The investment banks were left holding CODs they couldn't sell because the investors, tired of getting shafted, not only quit buying them, but because there had to be an ultimate end to the practice of selling serial mortgages on the same property.

Unsurprisingly, many of the newly-minted home owners quit paying their monthly payments as they had never had the money to do so in the first place, not to mention that the interest rates had spiked very quickly. To compound the issue, the economy tanked because of other government sinkholes like America's imperial escapades in Iraq, Afghanistan, and Northern Africa; wasteful foreign aid programs; and rising gas prices due to the depreciation of the US dollar.

But the crime spree didn't stop there. As Bear Stearns fell apart, Merrill Lynch was on the verge of falling apart and AIG fell, certain companies who had engaged in the same fraud and gambling continued to do well. This was because during the entire scam, the Federal Reserve was secretly giving trillions of dollars of no-interest loans to European banks, Bank of America, and still others with political connections Even though Bank of America's biggest boast was that it had not received bailout money from the government, it still managed to accept 1.344 trillion dollars from the Federal Reserve in secret. Citigroup accepted 2.513 trillion dollars. Yet these two were the top lending institutions during the housing bubble.

Bank of America (let's just call them BoA for brevity's sake) used their totally-not-bailout money to buy out Countrywide, one of their chief competitors. Countrywide not only created $97 billion worth of subprime mortgages, it also got a government bailout which it used to bankroll lavish bonuses. BoA's acquisition of Countrywide, purchased with money it got from the Fed, allowed them to expand their monopoly.

They ate Countrywide for pennies on the dollar while absorbing their government bailout, and then went on to acquire Merrill Lynch. Merrill Lynch had also received money from the Fed, which means that BoA ultimately benefited from that as well. On top of all of that, BoA received $30 billion in TARP money as well (totally not bailout money), which they subsequently spent on bonuses for themselves.

As a result of the Wall Street Reform and Consumer Protection Act, there was a one-time limited Government Accountability Office

(GAO) audit of the Federal Reserve. According to the GAO audit,

$16.1 trillion in secret loans were made by the Federal Reserve between December 1, 2007 and July21, 2010. It is not known how much they have spent between then and now. Forbes ran the title, "The Fed's $16 Trillion Bailouts Under-Reported".[8] And although it was reported by financial and business magazines like Forbes, it also wasn't making any headlines on the multi-headed beast that is ABCNNBCBS-FOX. Then again, these are the same networks which successfully sold the public on the idea of "too big to fail."

Bill Still, maker of The Money Masters and Jekyll Island: the Movie reported on Boiling Frogs Post that al of the three-letter networks had been themselves loaned out lock, stock and barrel to J.P. Morgan. As he told me in a past interview, "They rely entirely on J.P. Morgan rolling over their loans. If J.P. Morgan did not roll over their loans, the network(s) would be out of business in a week."[9] The following list of firms and the amount of money that they received was taken directly from page 131 of the Government Accountability Office audit report!

Government Accountability Office Audit Report

Citigroup	$2.513 trillion
Morgan Stanley	$2.041 trillion
Merrill Lynch	$1.949 trillion
Bank of America	$1.344 trillion
Barclays PLC	$868 billion
Bear Sterns	$853 billion
Goldman Sachs	$814 billion
Royal Bank of Scotland	$541 billion
J.P. Morgan Chase	$391 billion
Deutsche Bank	$354 billion
UBS	$287 billion
Credit Suisse	$262 billion
Lehman Brothers	$183 billion
Bank of Scotland	$181 billion
BNP Paribas	$175 billion
Wells Fargo	$159 billion
Dexia	$159 billion
Wachovia	$142 billion
Dresdner Bank	$135 billion
Societe Generale	$124 billion
"All Other Borrowers"	$2.639 trillion

Table from page 131 of the 2011 "United States Government Accountability Office: Report To Congressional Addressees"[10].

Bank of America tried to lie to our faces by claiming that they hadn't receive any bailout money when in fact they were getting money from the Fed all along. The Fed created the bouncing interest rates and rather than do something to stop it, helped facilitate it. The Security and Exchange Commission was asleep at the wheel, and no court on any level has done anything worth getting excited about.

And instead of all of this being massive news, instead of reporting about the biggest fraud of this century, the first thing the media did after the GAO audit came out was to completely ignore it and instead entertain the masses with Charlie Sheen's hedonistic lifestyle, the rise and fall of "Tom-Kat"[2] and other useless distraction pieces. Remember again that it was this same media which sold the public on the line, "too big to fail." Each talking head looked in the camera and explained in confident, soothing tones how the government bailouts had been necessary. "Too big to fail," became as much of a catch-phrase tool of the media as "weapons of mass destruction" had been in the build-up to the insane, unjustified invasion of Iraq just a few years earlier.

People should be furious. The Fed secretly gave trillions of dollars to select banks and businesses, which not only helped them to buy up their competition but also any other companies that happened to catch their eye, thus enabling them to cement their control over even more powerful, incontestable monopolies.

This wasn't a failure of capitalism. This was a failure of government, which came about not as the result of a lack of regulation, but was the inevitable result of good old-fashioned, illegal collusion. Simply put, this was outright fraud. The rating agencies engaged in fraud through their faulty ratings; the investment banks, through their bribery of said

---

[2] This portmanteau referred at the time to celebrity couple Tom Cruise and Katie Holmes.

agencies and the subsequent hoodwinking of their investors. And the lending banks engaged in fraud throughout the falsification of documents, or in some cases, by simply not requiring any documents at all.

The whole process was phony. Look at the people whose homes they are foreclosing on now: we now know that some of them had, in fact, paid their mortgages, even though the official books say they didn't. The system was automated, and it would seem that a gaggle of imbeciles was left to run the programs. (Just a heads-up: if you're told that your house must be foreclosed on and you ask to see the paperwork, odds are they might not have it.)

Obviously there never should have been bailouts in the first place; if you have engaged in fraud, you deserved to fail. But since there was, it would have at least made sense to earmark the money so that it would be spent on something constructive, like refinancing mortgages. Unfortunately, that didn't happen because Obama was anti-earmark and preferred the blank-check method of trusting corporations to be benevolent. All that really ended up happening was that all the crooks got rewarded with bonuses. There were two $700 billion bailouts on Obama's watch, plus TARP, plus Obama's stimulus package – all of which were really only fancy-talk to justify even more massive government spending on pork projects. The only thing they really ended up stimulating was the national debt.

These investment bankers not only deserved to fail, they belonged in jail. Allowing counterfeiters to gamble with other people's money engenders a system of deception. This is why the more honest financial experts refer to these bankers in their commentaries as "banksters".

The press shouldn't be let off the hook either. While they uniformly and obediently repeated the state's official message and excuses to the public, they somehow failed to report on the 16-trillion dollar secret bailout awarded by the Federal Reserve. There were only a few people on the air who had the courage and integrity to bring it up: Judge Andrew Napolitano, Dylan Ratigan and Ben Swann. And despite gathering the best ratings, none of them are on the air any longer. Napolitano went on to write a best- seller called Lies the Government Told You.[11] Ratigan wrote his own best-selling book called Greedy Bastards.[12]. Ben Swann has started his own independent media site.[13]

CHAPTER 4

So Just Tax the Rich, Right?

"The people are hungry: it is because those in authority eat up too much in taxes."

– Lao Tzu

So why can't we just tax rich people more? Sadly, the belief that tax money will somehow be automatically, graciously redistributed to the poor is a myth. The government spends over half of the discretionary taxes it receives on the military (and of that, most of it goes to shiny, new war toys, not the salaries of the soldiers). Furthermore higher taxes can mean businesses simply move out of the country.

As long as the US government continues to waste hundreds of billions of dollars on wars and occupations, not to mention spend more on its military than Russia, China, India, Germany, Japan, France and the United Kingdom combined, taxing people more won't solve a thing. All it will accomplish is to make the next war we engage in larger and more expensive.

Before we can enact any new taxes or tax increases, we must first embrace a healthy dose of rationality and enact some spending cuts. Every time the government complains about the budget deficit or national debt, we should all respond by demanding some appropriate cuts in defense spending. And let's be totally clear: what the government prefers to label "defense" is, in reality, offense. The barbaric actions of both the military and the Central Intelligence

Agency (CIA) so far have served only to encourage rather than discourage the violent reactions of countries with which we engage. And yet every time Congress whines about the need to raise the debt ceiling, they pretend like the only other options are to cut social programs or raise taxes. It's all hogwash used to hide the untouchable mass of military pork.

While they are audacious enough to evoke the name of our troops to justify more military spending, the reality is that the troops are not seeing any of the money either. Contracts are actually going out to weapons manufactures to build new military vehicles for the troops which have been discovered to be incredibly unsafe. Some of them do not even work at all because they are designed around the most expensive components rather than the most combat effective.

So when our congressmen cry that they don't have enough money to cover our domestic needs, it falls to the public to step up and demand an end to the pointless wars, bloated military budget, and highly immoral, costly activities of our intelligence and security agencies. Whenever the government throws up a scare tactic, it is up to us to have the presence of mind to see through it.

Governments love a good crisis. As President Obama's former White House Chief of Staff Rahm Emanuel stated, "You never want a serious crisis to go to waste. And what I mean by that [is] it's an opportunity to do things you think you could not do before."[14] One can only stand in awe at the three- letter network coined "fiscal cliff" fiasco of 2012-

2013. The government alleges to have saved us from this fiscal cliff crisis, a rescue it accomplished through the creation of all-new methods of legalized theft. The fact is this crisis was a self-inflicted one, brought about through reckless over-spending, mostly on murdering foreigners, and hidden behind the disingenuous rubric of the "war on terror".

The other giant sinkhole remains the US government's policy of selective corporate welfare, which has been presented to the public as a necessary step to be taken to avoid a crisis. Our government spends an incredible amount of money helping the public afford things that the government itself helped make unaffordable to begin with.

However, there is a camp out there that is blind to all of this. They do not blame the government for wasting money, but the wealthy for not paying enough taxes. "If only we taxed rich people more everything would be fine, and rainbows would shoot out of all the mail boxes!" they claim. If I had a dime for every time I heard someone blame the entire economic depression on the Bush-era tax cuts, I could afford to make Warren Buffet my butler. And for the sake of historical accuracy, it was President Obama who made the Bush tax cuts permanent,[15] so we ought to be calling them the Obama tax cuts now.

So how can taking money away from the producers and employers and giving it to the totally honest, benevolent, peace-loving leaders in Washington be bad for the economy? The problem is that there aren't any honest, benevolent, peace-loving leaders in Washington; just the usual crowd of dishonest, malevolent, war-mongering yes-men. They don't lift a finger to redistribute wealth to help the poor.

Rather, they do the exact opposite: they take money away from the average citizen and hand it over to Wall Street speculators so they might better engage in fraud, and to the Pentagon so they might better engage in mass murder. Considering where our tax money ends up, why in the world would you want the government to have even more of it? As it is, our existing social welfare suffers from the age-old problem where the majority of the money allotted winds up being eaten by the administrative fees of middlemen.

Welfare is supposed to be a safety-net that support people after they lose a job long enough to find a new one. The programs were not designed to have people remain on them for years and years. However they are designed with disincentives for people to get off of them. When a person on welfare does start to earn a little bit of money then all their benefits can be threatened. Benefit cliffs can prevent people from taking a transitional job that would be necessary for creating better earnings over time. People working the lower end jobs have great resentment for those earning the around same amounts who stay home.

There will always be a division between those satisfied to live as freeloader and those who want to work. Why work a minimum wage job if you can make the same amount of money collecting welfare and enjoying copious amounts of leisure time? Most people not only wouldn't, they don't, making reliable employees hard to find. An obvious solution would be to pay more than the minimum wage requires. But wages are not arbitrary; one has to produce more than what they are paid or they simple won't be hired. If good cost a store 5 dollars and they sell them for ten, then an employee making $10 an hour, needs to sell $20 worth of product just for the owner to break even. And this must be maintained for every hour and every employee throughout the day. This also ignores the lease on the building, the electric, the taxes, heating, and all the other costs that come with owning a business. In the case of America's biggest corporate franchises, the minimum wage law protect them from new competitors. Start up businesses rely on rapid turnover before they start really making profits however the extended time this may take might outweigh the initial needed for payroll. When companies have to pay employees' expensive healthcare that seems like a plus but it just decreases the chances of the employee ever getting a raise.

There will always be legitimate and illegitimate cases in welfare; one can always cherry-pick the examples he wishes to support his case. Yet talking about how much money is spent on helping the poor, freeloading or genuinely in need of help, is a moot point. Our system of safety-net welfare can't hold a candle to the behemoth that is corporate welfare. One ought to be far more disgusted and angry at the millionaires and billionaires receiving stupefying amounts of tax money from the government. Prioritize your lists. There is nothing the government enjoys more than creating division and fighting amongst the hoi polloi while the plutocrats get off scot-free.

When it comes to socio-economic issues, this continues to be a continuing source of aggravation between progressives and libertarians. The progressive will say things like, "So you just want to throw everyone out into the street?" or, "Corporations can just do whatever they want with no regulations? That's corporatism!" The great misunderstanding progressives have about libertarians and non-interventionist policy has nothing to do with the foreign policy of peace and trade. They support peace at least when their own particular brand is not in charge. Conversely, they'll tolerate more war just as long as the perception that the government is taking care of the poor persists.

They would rather tax everyone, especially corporations and the rich, and give that money to their imaginary benevolent overlords in DC, who will then, out of the goodness of their hearts, redistribute it to the needy, rather than drop 708 billion dollars into the defense department to allow them to perfect their program of mass murder. Just say the war is humane and you can sell enough of them on it and win their support. Likewise, all you have to do is just say that foreign and domestic aid is helping the poor and they will believe you.

What the majority of progressives do not understand is that corporatism exists because of government, not in spite of it. Where do corporate welfare and bailouts come from? They come from the government. It comes in the form of defense contracts, or it might just be a direct bailout. Without the government and the Fed, you can't have either one.

The only way the government can create jobs is by taking resources away from the private sector, which ironically means fewer jobs remain in the private sector. To encourage true wealth sharing, perhaps the government ought to offer a tax cut for those with higher   payrolls. Instead we have the opposite situation, where the payroll tax just makes less money available for employees and the businesses they work for, but more for the government. Hamilton Nolan had this to say about it in Gawker:

The people who can afford to pay more should pay more. The payroll tax represents the opposite of this idea. It only applies to the first $110K in earnings. That way, it makes sure to capture a significant portion of the earnings of all poor-to-middle-class people, and then cut off before capturing a significant portion of the earnings of any rich people.

It specifically is attacking the poor, as most people do not earn $110k a year anyway. And: If you are a full time fast food worker making, say, minimum wage—$7.25 per hour, 40 hours a week, 50 weeks per year—you make $14,500 per year, or $290 per week. More than six percent of that is taken out of your check right off the top for payroll taxes. If you are a full time CEO making $14.5 million per year, you also pay a little over six percent—except, not on the last $14.4 million per year. [16]

However, when you bring up the topic of tax cuts for businesses, you will find a significant portion of the working class is ideologically opposed to them, as they work under the belief that all business are greedy and want to avoid paying any taxes at all. As a result they fight against any breaks for businesses, not understanding that they are working against their own best interests. What they fail to understand is that one significant tax for businesses is the payroll tax, which has to be cut out of an employee's paycheck, theoretically to fund social security.

The London School of Economics was quoted in the same article: The payroll tax cut, which was in place during all of 2011 and 2012, reduced Social Security and Medicare taxes withheld from workers' paychecks by 2 percent. This tax cut affected nearly 155 million workers in the United States, and put an additional $1,000 a year in the pocket of an average household earning $50,000. As part of the 'fiscal cliff' negotiations, Congress allowed the 2011-12 payroll tax cut to expire at the end of 2012, and the higher income that workers had grown accustomed to was gone.

Yet worst of all the money they take from workers for their social security isn't actually saved for social security. The government spends it on other things. Yes they spent all 2.6 trillion of it. Charles Krauthammer explained this in the Washington Post:

When your FICA tax is taken out of your paycheck, it does not get squirreled away in some lockbox in West Virginia where it's kept until you and your contemporaries retire. Most goes out immediately to pay current retirees, and the rest (say, $100) goes to the U.S.Treasury – and is spent. On roads, bridges, national defense, public television, whatever – spent, gone. In return for that $100, the Treasury sends the Social Security Administration a piece of paper that says: IOU $100. There are countless such pieces of paper in the lockbox. They are called 'special issue' bonds. [17]

South Carolina Senator Earnest Hollings revealed to the Federal Reserve Chairman what Congress had actually been doing with the money, which is supposed to be in an untouchable trust (emphasis added):

What we've been doing, Mr. Chairman, in all reality, is taken a
hundred billion out of the Social Security Trust Fund, transferring it
over to the spending column, and spending it. Our friends to the left
here are getting their tax cuts, we are getting our spending increases,
and hollering surplus, surplus, and balanced budget, and balanced
budget plans when we continue to spend a hundred billion more than
we take in.[18]

So just to sum up: the government is lying and stealing. Imagine my
lack of shock. The government has been lying to people and stealing
their money from the Social Security trust. They continue to finance
this theft by collecting even more money from the public with the
promise that it will be kept safe and sound in that trust, to be returned
to them when they retire.

One might say that the government has a reverse Midas touch, which
causes everything they get involved in to lose value. Education,
energy, agriculture, healthcare, housing, foreign aid, the environment,
even the mail; everywhere they try to help the people, they end up just
making things more expensive for them. While it may not be what
progressives intended, this outcome is dictated by the realities of
economics. A new bubble is coming, but this time it will be the debt
bubble. The nation's debt is already enormous and the government
cannot go on borrowing forever.

The freedom we should have is the freedom to be responsible for our
own actions. It is a tendency of human nature that we try to make laws
not for ourselves, but for other people. People think that by placing
restrictions on other people, they are doing it for their own good and
protection. But the government must stay out of issues of economic
equality and personal liberty, because to do otherwise always results
in tyranny. The erosion of civil liberties coincides with the tyranny
of government, which always begins its expansion quietly hidden
behind do-gooder labels. No one should get bent out of shape over

what they think their neighbor does with their own body, or how they spend their money. If you feel the overpowering urge to do so, just take a deep breath and then grow up.

Beware of the resentful. Many Liberals don't really care about the poor so much as they just hate the rich. Conservatives don't hate the poor, they just hate losing money.

CHAPTER 5

Education

"Unfortunately our education system is not only failing to teach critical thinking, it is often itself a source of confused rhetoric and emotional venting in place of systematic reasoning."

– Thomas Sowell

When the government subsidizes higher education, it accomplishes nothing but to make it more expensive. Given that universities not only partner with but also invest in defense companies, the government, through its student loan program, has managed to create an ingenuous system to launder money through the universities and into the war industry. The schools, knowing they can count on these guaranteed loans, hike tuition costs at their convenience.

This has resulted in rapidly inflating costs, which in turn make it increasingly more difficult to go to school without getting a loan – with interest, of course. But shouldn't everyone go to college? The problem now is that there is practically no one who can afford it anymore. Today's students graduate with the equivalent debt of a large mortgage, but without the benefit of a house to go with it.

Schools waste a lot of money on things that they claim support education. They spend the money on campus beautification projects. They dump it into landscaping, or state-of-the-art facilities for extracurricular activities. Colleges have become businesses driven by profit.

There is hardly a college in the United States that doesn't play the parking permit gambit, wherein it sells more parking passes than there are available parking spaces. Every morning it becomes a game of musical chairs, where he who arrives last is forced to park illegally in order to avoid being late for class, or even missing it entirely. This system of over-selling may profit the school, but means that on any given day there will be a large number students stuck paying for a parking ticket.

There exists a similar scam in the textbook industry, where every year a new edition of a textbook is required for a class, even though in reality only a line or two has been changed from the previous one. This artificially accelerated flood of revisions forces each year's crop of new students to pay full price for new editions, often costing hundreds of dollars per book, while preventing former students from recouping some of their investment in the used-book market. If the primary concern of universities is for education and not profit, then why do their faculty members allow this to be done to their students?

Unfortunately, this situation has become the rule, not the exception. Only a few schools remain where students have organized themselves, e.g. in online forums, as a way to facilitate the continuing resale of old books when feasible, and also to circumvent this planned obsolescence.

Such scams pale, however, when compared to the worst of the travesties perpetrated on students today. Many universities have begun withholding students' transcripts in order to punish them for outstanding student loan payments. Professor Andrew Ross of the website Occupy Student Debt[19]   has this to say of the practice:

It's worse than indentured servitude. With indentured servitude, you had to pay in order to work, but then at least you got to work. When universities withhold these transcripts, students who have been indentured by loans are being denied even the ability to work or to finish their education so they can repay their indenture.

What justification does a school have to withhold their students' transcripts when the school itself has already been paid? The balance on the loan is owed to the lender, be it either a private bank or the government, not the school.

The LA Times explained the reasoning behind this policy when they reported:

It's no accident that colleges are using the withholding of official transcripts to punish students behind in their loan payments. It turns out the federal government encourages the practice. Schools are not required by law to withhold transcripts, but a spokeswoman at the Department of Education confirmed that the department 'encourages' them to use the draconian tactic, saying that the policy 'has resulted in numerous loan repayments.

It is a strange position for colleges to take, however, since the schools themselves are not owed any money Student loan funds come from private banks or the federal government. For federal Perkins loans, schools get a pool of federal money to apply to students' financial aid, and if students don't pay, that pool gets smaller. But the creditor is still the government, not the college. And in the case of so-called Stafford loans, schools are not on the hook in any way; they are simply acting as collection agencies, and in fact may get paid for their efforts atcollection.[20]

The fewer students pay back their loans, or the more slowly they pay, the smaller the available pool of new loan money becomes for the universities to use for their new or currently enrolled students. By fixing the pool of available loan money for each school, the government creates an incentive for the school to get involved in the payment-collection process. Offsetting the burden of debt collection onto the universities thus creates a moral hazard whereby universities are encouraged to act ruthlessly against their graduates to secure future funding through the loan system.

Most college graduates now finish school with a massive debt that they will likely spend decades repaying. Interest kills, and in some of these debts the students have been given interest payments that exceed the principal of the initial loan. The result is a new socio-economic class of educated debt slaves.

While economics might seem boring, it probably has more real-world applications for the majority of the population than most of the curriculum taught in public schools nowadays. Perhaps if more of today's college students had been taught some basic economics in high school, they might not have been so eager to burden themselves with exorbitant college loans that will take them the majority of their adult lives to pay back.

* * *

When it comes to lower education, our public school system is just as plagued by a similar, for-profit industry entrenched in government. We all want to help people, especially the poor, to do better in school Oh, here's an idea! We can just give the schools more money, right? However, giving money to schools is not as straightforward as distributing welfare to the poor. It does not help those whose problems in school stem from problems at home, which themselves often come from financial stress on the families. Throwing money at schools is an attempt at a solution that has already been repeated time and time again. Unfortunately, it simply doesn't work. Schools, like any government body, will quickly find ways to tie up their budget increases in administrative costs, pointless landscaping projects, and/or massive kickback scams involving the purchase of texts books etc.

According to 2006 data from the US Department of Education, only 35% of American high school seniors are proficient in reading, and 23% in math. On the global stage, America ranks last in educational effectiveness among large industrialized countries despite the highest spending-per-student ratio in the world.

Teacher unions are bitterly opposed to a voucher system, not to mention the creation of charter schools. Public schools enjoy an enrollment system based on zip codes. Most people do not have a choice where their children can go to school unless they have enough money to send them to a private school. As a result, the public schools are scared to death of competition.

A voucher system essentially creates a scholarship for people who cannot afford private school. If you simply disbursed money for schooling directly to families, there would be no guarantee that it would actually go towards the students' education. Disbursed as a voucher, however, guarantees that 100% of its value is spent on sending the student to the school of his or her choice. The hope is that the existence of real competition may force public schools into performing better. Due to the traditional tenure system, it is so costly to fire a bad teacher in the public school system that less than one-third of one percent of them are let go, no matter how poor or criminal their performances are.[21]

On a per-student basis, the US out-spends every nation in the world on education, and yet is nowhere near the top in proficiency in any subject. Some US schools are spending over $18,000 per student. [22]

That's a lot of tax money. But where is it all going? When you look at these classrooms, it's hard to figure out just where the annual sticker price is actually being spent. New Jersey spent thirty-one billion dollars in a single decade for just 31 school districts.

The premise they were working under was that the best way to fix the schools in poor neighborhoods was to just spend more money. There were over ten schools getting over three hundred thousand a year for each class; some were over four hundred thousand. Yet the average teacher's salary was only fifty-five thousand, and these were people who usually prepared and taught multiple subjects. It doesn't take a mathematician to realize that the majority of the money must have gone to administrative costs, which in fact usually came in at about ninety cents on the dollar.

Such administrative costs are excessive, to say the least. Bill Baroni, a state senator from New Jersey (which happens to be the state which spends the most on education in the US), points out that they have over 400 administrators making more than a hundred thousand dollars a year – and that in Newark alone. Superintendents are giving themselves severance packages that, when combined with their pensions, come in just shy of a million dollars. The problem is that the average person will support unconditionally any money that claims to be for education. Thus it created a cartel capable of robbing the public blind because their association with the very mention of education grants them an air of impunity.

* * *

Another problem in modern education has been the attack on imagination in schools, which has led to a new form of moral decay in our society. Many people can no longer answer such simple questions as, "Why aren't we more kind to one another?" or "Why do people kill each other?"

These are questions even a five-year old child should be able to answer. Yet we now live in a society where such basic exercises as putting oneself in another person's shoes, imagining the consequences of one's actions on the environment, or considering the depletion of over-exploited resources, has fallen by the wayside. As a result, it should come as no surprise that we wind up living in a self-gratifying, self- centered shell of the now.

Imagination is not just some fantastic device to be used for a child's entertainment, complete with purple dragons and storybook princesses. Empathy and sympathy both stem from imagination. The foolish, false dichotomy of pitting imagination against rational thought has been poisonous for the humanities.

This might explain how we can be smart enough to invent the nuclear bomb, a mind-boggling array of guided missiles, and the unmanned drone, and then be stupid enough to actually employ them. The amount of scientific brainpower poured into these projects has been both enormous and impressive. The staggering lack of thought currently put into developing a child's sense of humanity – the same sense which is supposed to guide our judgment in everyday matters like, "perhaps there's another option besides incinerating that city with giant fireballs?" – is truly frightening.

Richard Feynman, who worked on building the first atomic bombs dropped on Japan, stated that his initial reason for working on the project was out of the fear that if we could build it so could the Germans. That's why we had to finish it first. He went on to say that when the reason changed (after Germany had been defeated), he did not go back to address the moral question of whether they should continue building the bomb. The work simply continued. His defense? "I simply didn't think, OK?"[23] This was a man of extraordinary genius who was by no means a wicked person. Such is the cognitive dissidence that can be created by war, aided and abetted by the lopsided mental training, devoid of moral philosophy, which we now teach in our schools.

The attack on imagination in schools, where is treated as if it were some sort of useless, evolutionary holdover to be overcome, has proven disastrous. There is nothing frivolous about being imaginative, just as there is nothing heartless about being rational. These are both good and necessary qualities that should carry no stigma, nor be treated as conflicting qualities. Our best science has come from those who were as imaginative as they were technical. We should embrace imagination and not only foster it in our children, but continue to foster it in our adults.

Within the current government-run school system, the goal of education seems to be to instill obedience and the ability to retain a random collection of facts – long enough to pass a standardized test, anyway. Students get depressed over the resulting impractical, time-consuming busy-work, which eats away at the hours of their youth. But perhaps there is another motivation behind this lobotomization of our imaginations, one which can best be conveyed through the words of the great Ron Swanson:[3] "Give a man a fish and you feed him for a day, don't teach a man to fish and you feed yourself."

The current educational model seems to be designed to drown students in mountains of useless, abstract academic minutiae, hamstring them with decades of debt, withhold teaching them applicable skills for the workplace, and then set them loose into the real world to fend for themselves. That the modern, universally accepted definition of the "real world" now seems equate to "not in school anymore" should tell us just how divorced our modern method of education is from the actual knowledge and skills we need to cope with real life.

Then there is what President Bush called, "the bigotry of low expectations," where by standards for admission for higher education are categorically lower for some groups than others. The left's

---

[3] A fictional character played by Nick Offerman on the American sitcom TV series, Parks and Recreation

identitarian obsession with equality of outcome has created racist policies, ironically in the name of fighting racism. Asians must have higher test scores than Whites who must have higher scores than Hispanics and Blacks to attend the same school.[24] This policy is bad for everyone. Blacks have their credibility undermined, Asians may not get into the school of their choice despite being the best qualified, and worse of all it sets up a state recognized acknowledgment of horrible racial stereotypes.

* * *

The final problem worth mentioning is the trend towards making test scores the ultimate measure of education. Doing so means that some places will make teaching the test the goal of the curriculum, rather than actual subject matter. After all, if they were to get lower scores than dictated by the parameters of the test, some folks might just move their kids into a private school. Then again, if you start awarding failure (that is to say the school gets more money when they do poorly and has it taken away when they do well), you're creating a system where you're just subsidizing failure. Bob Bowdon made an excellent documentary called The Cartel, which further explains what is wrong with public education in America.[25]

CHAPTER 6

Agriculture and Energy

"Nobody is qualified to become a statesman who is entirely ignorant of the problem of wheat."

– Socrates

When the government subsidizes alternative energy, all it really ends up accomplishing is to drive up its price. It has placed so many conditions on the utilization of natural energy sources that it has become impossible to afford them without the aid of a government grant.

Here is an anecdotal example: I wanted to install a wind turbine for my house in North Carolina. I ultimately had to give up on the idea due to the sheer mass of government paperwork that it entailed, coupled with the huge risk I would be taking if any of the subsequent, necessary grants did not come through.

While the government was willing to pay for 75% of the cost, they had also managed to force that cost 80% higher than it had previously been. That means every person who went through with buying a turbine would end up an accomplice in squandering an enormous sum in taxpayer dollars. And for what? Previous to government involvement, folks had been able to buy the same equipment for far less money, and without spending a dime from the taxpayer's coffers.

Other government-mandated programs instituted in the name of renewable energy have been disastrous, too. Take corn-derived ethanol, for example. Why wasn't the market allowed to choose what to turn into ethanol, and for how much? Why not use sugar cane, as they do in Brazil? Why not use soy or hemp?

Industrial hemp offers the cheapest source of ethanol with the highest potential yield per acre, yet is demonized in the US for its superficial relation to marijuana. Out of all the options available, corn is by far the worst option we could have chosen.

The ratio of petroleum-based fuel needed to make a gallon of ethanol-based fuel is about 1 to 1.1, with an associated 10% reduction in the corn crop available for animal feed and human food. Compared to any other crop that might be used to produce ethanol, corn is by far the most resource-hungry, both in terms of land acreage and water usage. This doesn't make ethanol as an alternative fuel a bad idea by any means but does highlight the severity of the mistake we made in allowing the government to dictate the rules of ethanol production on our behalf. The decades-old system of farm subsidies for the corn/corn syrup industry has caused enough problems already, without the addition of this new complication.

Mismanagement of crops isn't the only problem plaguing American agriculture. Food animals are now being raised on so-called factory farms, a form of farming encouraged by the subsidy system. This has created such harsh living conditions that a new market for antibiotics has sprung up just to keep the animals raised there from dying of bad diets, disease and infection. Pigs are packed like sardines into crowded, unspeakably filthy pens, which not only increase the possibility of creating new super-strain diseases, but also threaten to ruin downstream estuaries as well.

The drugs for the animals, normally unnecessary but for the cramped living conditions are conveniently purchased with money from farm subsidies (i.e. taxpayer money). These drugs are usually purchased from select drug companies with business ties to the politicians that write the laws. In modern American ranching, livestock animals are now pumped full of antibiotics from the time of their birth to the slaughter house. As a matter of fact, 70% of the antibiotics made in the US are administered not to humans, but to the animals they consume.[26]

That is a lot of drugs. Chemicals now considered standard for farming/ranching include not only antibiotics, but also steroids used to make animals bigger, pesticides sprayed on crops, and preservatives mixed into the final products from each. As a result, farm subsidies for Big Ag now also serve as an indirect subsidy for Big Pharma.

The food created from these subsidies is helping to make less healthy Americans, especially among the poor, whose supermarket purchase strategy consists mainly of buying whatever is cheapest at the time. But Big Pharma doesn't mind big people, because the more health problems there are, the more money there is to be made in selling the medicines they need to stay alive.

The Midwest states, which are the agribusiness centers of the country, control a huge block of senators on both sides of the aisle. As a result, neither party will raise a finger to object to the situation that has developed.

Farm subsidies are now among the most untouchable of subjects (like aid to Israel, or military spending). And it's not just the drug companies. A long list of seemingly unrelated industries (cosmetics, heavy machinery, tobacco, lumber, fast-food chains) are also benefiting indirectly through the farm subsidy system via an artificial demand for their products, which has been created by the inhumane living conditions of the factory farms.

It is almost as if the government were attempting to funnel money directly to the drug and chemical companies. Perhaps that's why the government agency responsible for overseeing all of this has been unironically dubbed the Food and Drug Administration (FDA); regardless of whether the companies under their purview make food or drugs, they're all on the same team.

* * *

So perhaps you decide to distance yourself from this mess and take some initiative. You might choose to grow your own food; buy directly from a local producer; try to raise public awareness by taking photos of a factory farm,[27] or heaven forbid, drink some raw milk![28]   Do so, though, and you might find yourself on a terrorist watch list, or even in jail. Such criminalization of citizen intervention leaves the field wide open for giant conglomerates like Monsanto, one of the largest corporations in the genetically- modified food industry. This is the very same corporation that made Agent Orange, the infamous chemical weapon that the American military dumped all over Indo-China during the Vietnam War. Now it has turned its interests to domestic pursuits, like producing genetically-modified (GM) food products, and cotton.

The question is, is GM food really that bad? Sometimes the results of genetic tinkering have the desired superior traits looked for, such as the ability to repel insects. But in many cases they have been shown to yield inferior crops, require more water to grow, and gradually lose the very traits they were designed for, which could have other, unforeseen long-term side effects. And there should be at least a modicum of concern that the former president of McDonald's, Janice L Fields, as well as the former CEO of Sara Lee, C. Steven McMillan, both sit on the Monsanto's board of directors. Isn't there a small conflict of interest when some of the largest volume purchasers of simple and processed foods also end up working for the largest genetically modified food giant?

At least they are only former employees of major monopolies; also present is Jon R. Moeller, the CFO of former food giant, P&G. More disturbing (not to mention just a little too reminiscent of its chemical-weapon producing days) is the presence of Robert Stevens, chairman of the board for Lockheed Martin.[29]

One might also feel concern as to why the government has consistently attempted to exclude these pillars of industry from any and all lawsuits directed towards them. With all of these corporate fat cats and their overlapping interests sitting on one board, perhaps it simply becomes very hard to tell them no. When Monsanto's cotton failed in India because it required far more water to maintain than natural cotton, a lot of Indian farmers lost everything they owned.[30] But which side do you think won out: the farmers, or the company with the all-star board of directors?

* * *

It seems one can't have a discussion about energy nowadays without touching on the subject of nuclear power. It turns out that one of the historically lesser- known facts about atomic energy is that there are multiple ways to generate it. Many alternative methods exist to what we use now, which also happen to be safer, cheaper, and friendlier to the environment (not to mention, to the humans that live in it). In regards to the United States, however, it long ago set upon an path of achieving nuclear energy, and all for the very non-scientific reason of bolstering the political support of a couple of local congressmen.

In 1972, Richard Nixon had the opportunity to choose in favor of the development of thorium-derived nuclear energy,[31] rather than the now-standard uranium or plutonium method. Thorium, the lesser-known relative of its more radioactive cousins, has considerable advantages over them. The most important factor is that the reactors that utilize it don't need water as a coolant. They also don't need to run at the high pressures that uranium or plutonium plants do.

This means they aren't in danger of the fallout associated with a plant explosion, nor do they require the construction of the huge buildings necessary to contain such a hazard. In addition, because thorium plants do not require water cooling, they don't need to be built near large bodies of water. Such a reactor could have especially benefited Japan in terms of preventing the 2011 Fukushima disaster, as they would never have needed to build a single reactor on the coast, subject to the threat of a tsunami.

Since thorium plants could be built wherever they're most beneficial, this would also eliminate the need to build and maintain the long transit lines necessary for transporting the generated electricity. Unlike uranium thorium doesn't need solid fuel, either, meaning that there is no risk of melt-down. Not only does it occur four times more abundantly in the earth's crust than uranium, it also generates hundreds of times less waste, and is by far a more efficient energy source than anything we have developed so far. In the state of Nevada alone, the US has over 32 metric tons of unused thorium in storage.

So despite all the obvious benefits of thorium, why did the United States instead decide to to single- mindedly invest in uranium-based energy technology? Because the people responsible for making the decision were less concerned with the science, economics, or future safety of the country than ensuring that they could use the associated technology investment to bring jobs to their home states.

In one phone conversation between President Nixon and Republican Congressman Craig Hosmer, he explained how he was going to pitch their plan to the public as a bipartisan effort. He told Hosmer that he had already come to an agreement with Democratic Congressman Chester Holifield, who was at the time chair of the Joint Committee on Atomic Energy and the Committee on Government Operations. During that conversation, Nixon told Congressman Hosmer, "Now this has got to be something we play close to the vest, but I have been ruthless on one thing. Any activity [for nuclear projects] that we possibly can should be placed in Southern California in this field and also in the saline water field. You know, we need jobs..And I decided to throw one big plant in California."[32] Their main concern was to play it close to the vest and pitch it as a bipartisan effort in order to use it to create jobs in California.

Naturally, Hosmer agreed with Nixon. It wasn't that he believed that the particular type of plant Nixon proposed was better, but that he appreciated the proposed location. President Nixon, Congressman Hosmer and Congressman Holifield – all from California – together realized the benefit creating such a giant public works project in their own backyard would bring. All in the name of creating jobs, of course. Their goal was not so much the longevity of the labor such a project would create, as it was the short-term goal of ensuring their own re-elections.

The other two congressmen (Holifield especially) were in the right position to squash any opposition. As a result, they managed to prevent thorium from going forward. It wasn't until Jimmy Carter that the US finally got its first thorium plant, and at that it was short-lived; it was shut down shortly after the Three Mile Island incident (a totally non-thorium related event). That didn't matter, of course. Nuclear power as a whole took a big hit in the arena of public opinion, and as a result, the public decided that it had to go.

Today, as India and China are both building new nuclear power plants, the US has decided to continue the use of fossil fuels for energy generation, no matter how many mountaintops they have to frack through to get to it. The cost to the environment, not to mention the treasury, will be incalculable. The incredible amounts of money that have been spent on the infrastructure to support it all would not have been necessary if the US had taken the more reasonable course and invested in thorium. The higher utility bills for the consumer that have resulted from the inefficiency of uranium-powered plants are all thanks to Nixon and his boys, and the cold decision they made that the best investment for them was to cater to California politics. The history of nuclear power in America is a true travesty, both economically and politically.

Perhaps, not surprisingly, there has been virtually no media coverage regarding the history of what happened. To this day, without the modern, widespread dissemination of hard-to-find information over the internet, there is a good chance you still wouldn't know that thorium existed, much less what it can do.[33]

Our decisions on land use for energy are not based on science or the public good but on political decisions influenced by the relationship of business and state. Hemp should replace corn for ethanol. Thorium should replace Uranium in nuclear energy. But market forces cannot do this while the state is protecting the failing, inferior industries.

CHAPTER 7

Flying the Federal Skies

"Those who surrender freedom for security will not have, nor do they deserve, either one."

– Benjamin Franklin

The modern experience of commercial flight in the US has become abysmal. The airline companies are finding new and creative ways to price-gouge, in the form of narrower seats, subpar food, and a new explosion in "optional fees" for things that used to be part of the service. Now the government has decided to pile on in the name of science and security, while showing a profound ignorance of both.

Have you ever wondered why it took the Federal Aviation Administration (FAA) so long to allow the use of electronic devices during flight? The common misconception that spawned the original ban was that the electronic interference created by such devices, most particularly those that broadcast voice and data, could interfere with the plane's critical systems and cause a crash. Apparently, though, different laws of physics govern in other countries, as I have never been asked to turn off my electronic devices on a domestic flight in Japan. As an additional bonus, I'm also not groped by the Transportation Security Administration (TSA), and can even bring my own beverages!

The real reason behind the blanket ban on phones, laptops, and other conveniences of modern technology was an ignorant, insane regulation cooked up by the bureaucratic thinking of the FAA. The reality is that there was no serious data to back it up. Think about it this way: if you could bring down a plane just by turning on your cell phone, just how long would it have taken for terrorists to realize that they could save themselves a lot of effort by bringing one on board and turning it on mid-flight? If such a tactic were viable, we would have had planes raining down out of the sky in a barrage of fiery carnage. Unlike the FAA, The terrorists were smart enough to realize that this wouldn't work. So much for the quality of education in America.

To be fair, though, it's not as though the FAA didn't offer a certification process to get an electronic device approved for in-flight operation. All an airline had to do to prove that an electronic device wouldn't interfere with a plane's systems was to make a single, passenger-free flight, carrying the specific make and model of the electronic device they want to test, and leave it turned on.

There was just one catch, though: the airline had to perform this test, one flight at a time, for each and every kind of device they wished to certify. This would have translated into making hundreds of flights; one for each model of iPhone, one for each model of Nokia, one each model of Android phone available, and so on. The same was required for every make and model of laptop, MP3 player, e-book reader and tablet. To say that the cost to the airlines would jump straight over "prohibitively expensive" and go straight to "insanely impractical" is an understatement. And so the ban continued.

Abby Lunardini, vice president of corporate communications at Virgin America, explained that the current guidelines require that an airline must test each version of a single device before it can be approved by the F.A.A. For example, if the airline wanted to get approval for the iPad, it would have to test the first iPad, iPad 2 and the new iPad, each on a separate flight, with no passengers on the plane.[34]

J. Mac McClellan, former editor and chief of Flying magazine, blogged his frustrations about how the FAA certification rules hurt us: Every pilot I know is frustrated by the capability of consumer electronics that is available for a few hundred bucks and can do more than FAA approved avionics costing many thousands. I know an iPad doesn't have the same level of testing and software documentation as the primary flight display (PFD) flat glass system certified for a piston airplane. But the iPad cost $300 to $500 and the PFD $10,000 for entry level. The cost gap, in this case, really can be blamed on FAA certification.[35] (sic)

He goes on to give an example of two systems, made by the same company, and virtually identical save for the difference in cost created by the level of certification required for each. This certification level was arbitrarily based on the weights of the planes the systems were intended for:

The G600 and G500 combined PFD/MFD systems look exactly the same, and with the same list of options, have the same capabilities. But the G600 costs more because some of its software is FAA approved to a higher level than in the G500. The FAA requires the higher level of software security and testing in airplanes weighing more than 6,000 pounds so Garmin has to charge more for the G600 to perform the same functions the as the G500. (sic)

Electronics manufacturers already go through stringent certification tests to meet electronics interference guidelines as laid out by the Federal Communications Commission (FCC). Commercial aircraft manufacturers go to significant lengths to shield critical systems from every type of radiation, be it from ground-based communications or the electromagnetic radiation of the sun. And yet the FAA continues to insist that they know best, based on a stubborn adherence to their own particular brand of institutional dogma.

The good news is that the FAA has finally lifted most of the restrictions for personal electronic devices, starting with e-book readers and tablets. But how did they suddenly come around to realize that these devices were suddenly safe? What was the purpose of maintaining their completely unscientific requirements for so long?

* * *

But this kind of eye-roll inducing ignorance is just a nuisance compared to the latest display of state- funded security theater that the government has decided to inflict on us. I'm referring to none other than that spawn of the Department of Homeland Security (DHS) which everyone loves to hate, the TSA.

While the TSA has never actually caught a terrorist, their policy of "everyone is a potential threat" has enabled them to waste a lot of taxpayer dollars and invade the privacy of millions. Their only real accomplishment has been to make air travel in the United States a special kind of hell.

Let me be blunt: the TSA is a useless organization. In test after test,[36] it has been shown that the security the TSA purports to offer can be circumvented. And the new, massive lines created by the TSA, where people are bunched together in zigzag formations, create a new and ironically excellent target for a would-be terrorist bomber or shooter.

Any motivated terrorist could walk in, surreptitiously drop a bag of rigged explosives next to an unsuspecting passenger, and then walk out again. A few minutes later the bomb goes off, kills hundreds of passengers in a single stroke, and prevents thousands more from flying out of the fear that airports are no longer safe. The terrorist would not even have to resign himself to the inevitable suicide that comes with taking over a plane. And what would the TSA's counter-solution to this new threat be? Make some sort of a line to pre-screen people before allowing them into the main line to be screened again? Then that line becomes the new terrorist's target and the cycle repeats.

The real reason for the existence of the TSA is that it has become an essential part of the security complex. The security complex uses scare tactics to get money for equipment and personnel from congress in much the same way the military- industrial complex does to get funding for research and manufacturing. They prey upon the knowledge that no one will argue that security is unnecessary. No one wants to be held responsible if someone gets hurt due to a perceived lack of it, so legislators cave in to every demand the security companies make. So the for-profit industries involved press their advantage in this regard to sell excessively overpowered hardware and draconian security measures. This has nothing to do with making you safer; it is about making them richer.

In 2010 was the Christmas Day bomber incident. A young man, Umar Farouk Abdulmutallab, allegedly hid a bomb inside his underwear. The circumstances around the incident are murky. It seems he was escorted by a well-dressed Indian man who told the ticket agent that Umar was from Sudan, that he didn't need a passport, and that they did this all the time. This exchange was witnessed by Kurt Haskell, a lawyer who happened to be in the waiting area at the time and whose attention had been drawn by the odd pair.

As it turns out, Umar was not from Sudan; he was from Nigeria. His father, Alhaji Umaru Abdulmutallab, is a Nigerian banker, and one of the richest men in Africa. He didn't manage to sneak past security with a bomb; he was welcomed onto the plane without a passport and with the cooperation of staff. The enforcement of normal procedures should have stopped him.

So who was this man escorting a terrorist onto a plane? Why wasn't there an investigation, or at least some effort made to find out who he was?

What we do know is who benefitted. Rapiscan, who made millions off of the sale of airport security scanners, has two parent companies: Optoelectronics Imaging Subsystems (OIS) and the Electronic Corporation of India, Ltd. (ECIL), the latter of which is run by the government of India. From 2007 to 2010 OIS's operation cash flow went from -2.3 million dollars to +54.2 million dollars, a difference of 56 million. From 2008 to 2009, ECIL went from -0.7 million to +44.5 million.

The middleman to sell the scanners was Michael Chertoff, the former head of the Department of Homeland Security. This is the same guy who allowed several 9/11 suspects to return to Israel; suspects who had not only failed their polygraph tests but had also been witnessed celebrating the attacks, and who happened to have worked for a foreign intelligence agency.

So we have two companies that just happen to have technology ready to go to protect us from the threat of an underwear bomb. One would think that getting contracts for machines that can look through your clothes, including your underwear, must be a pretty hard sell to make. But with the bombing attempt, the Chertoff Group had the perfect sales pitch for their clients' naked body scanners.

The TSA is under the umbrella of the DHS, which means what we have here is your typical revolving door, where a government official goes into the private sector only to starts peddling his wares back to his former colleagues at his old department. That there was an Indian man helping a terrorist get on a plane with a bomb is certainly no proof of the involvement of the Indian government or ECIL, but the fact that the US was not interested in investigating it does make the incident that much more suspicious.

* * *

Terrorist plots, while real, are sometimes manufactured for profit. This is nothing to scoff at. The CIA itself has fixed countless self-created disasters as a means of implementing US corporate policies abroad. The Federal Bureau of Investigation (FBI) has also been caught in one case of entrapment after another, where they go catch their own homemade crooks and then use them to justify or even increase their funding.

The US has covertly worked with other nations, such as Israel during the Iran-Contra affair,[37] to sell both illegal drugs and arms while fostering a civil war.

 Or with Pakistan, with whom they financed terrorist cells (which they called "freedom fighters") in Afghanistan to fight the Soviets. Making terrorists for financial benefit, or to harm US rivals, is nothing new, so the idea of India and the US working together to stage an event like the underwear bombing would not be so far-fetched, either. These kinds of things happen all the time. You can't sell mouse traps until someone has mice.

Someone sure made a lot of money on stocks for the airlines involved in the terrorist attacks of September 11th, 2001, too. It would serve the public well if the

Deposit Trust & Clearing Corporation (DTCC) were investigated for their part in enabling massive, naked short-selling in the stock market.[38] The DTCC knows who was selling airline stocks short just prior to 9/11. With multiple hedge fund managers winding up dead in their pools, and no trace on who was selling the naked shorts (all in the same week and for the same industries), there is no way of knowing whether or not some put options were placed with the

73

foreknowledge of future sabotage on industries they smothered in uncovered IOUs.[4]

Naked shorts sales are not only illegal, they make terrorist acts available for investment. Suspicious selling behavior can not only be seen during the collapse of Bear Stearns or Lehman Brothers at the climax of the subprime bubble roller coaster, but also in the sudden plummet of specific airline stocks just prior to the events of September 11th. The two airline stocks most affected by the September 11th terrorist attacks just happened to be the two airlines involved in the hijackings, United Airlines and American Airlines.

After the terrorist attacks, American Airline's stock price fell by 39 percent. And while the put-call ratio[39] for United Airlines was 25 times above normal on September 6, after the attacks the company's stock fell 42 percent. There were no similar trades on any other airlines. The SEC did launch an investigation, but without DTCC cooperation, the origins of the short sales remain unknown. Call options (betting that a certain stock's price will go up), were placed on weapons companies like Raytheon, which saw its stock price rise 37% the week the market re-opened after 9/11. While this is more than a little suspicious, it is still just circumstantial evidence, because you can't prove insider trading isn't just really, really good luck.

Did someone know those airline stocks would plummet? Is this connected to why the FAA shredded the taped account of 16 air-traffic controllers describing the events of 9/11, and of whom some had even talked to people on the hijacked planes? From a New York Times article published on May 6, 2004, "That manager crushed the cassette in his hand, shredded the tape and dropped the pieces into different

---

[4] A put option refers to a practice where investors bet that a stock will go down by a certain date (they don't actually buy the stock, just bet against it). See also "Put Option Definition". Investopedia.com. http://www.investopedia.com/terms/p/putoption.asp

trash cans around the building, according to a report made public today by the inspector general of the Transportation Department."[40]

The DTCC secretly hired hardline Israeli partisan, Gary Weiss, to write positive blogs about the DTCC, defend the practice of naked short-selling, and protect their Wikipedia page from critics. With its squeaky- wheel approach to editing and its tendency to appeal to the lowest common denominator, Wikipedia, despite its very official-sounding name (ending in "pedia"), is not always the best place to go to for the real facts of a situation.

The fact is, the DTCC is where all the financial institutions must route shorts and illegal naked shorts. And while Wikipedia may call it merely controversial it is in fact absolutely illegal. The DTCC has to have known who was shorting what and when, yet all that information remains confidential. If there is nothing to hide, then why hire a PR guy and give him a DTCC computer to publish rationalizations about the validity of uncovered short sales? Instead of making American citizens guilty until proven innocent, we should be using those funds to investigate the DTCC. If you'd like to know more about the DTCC and its role in protecting naked short sellers, check out this lecture.

* * *

If we really are concerned about security, then we need to look at the big fish: the intelligence agencies, usually American, which have managed out-killed all of the terrorist groups combined. Without US and Saudi support, most of the well-known terrorist groups around the world would not exist. Terrorist groups nowadays serve as the modern privateers of the state. This is why we need to take a long, hard look into the financing and motivation behind the terrorism, rather than our current policy of knee-jerk reaction to individual terrorist attacks.

In 2011, Congressman Ron Paul brought a bill before Congress called the American Traveler Dignity Act, which would have abolished the TSA's ability to ignore the 4th amendment. The bill never had a hearing, despite having the enthusiastic support of a majority of Americans. It never went to the floor because, although practically every congressman claims they dislike the TSA, they would have been forced to show their cards and vote it down, and thus be on the record as actually supporting the agency. So the bill died in committee, as bills often do.

But what motivation would members of Congress have to vote down a bill that would rein in the TSA? They knew that by doing so they would face the wrath of the American public. Yet they could not support the bill, either, because the TSA makes too much money for too many important people.

The fear of terrorism has changed American life in significant ways. It has become more expensive to travel. The government now harasses its own citizens on a daily basis in the name of stopping terrorism, yet continues its policy of militant aggression overseas, which have played a large role in making America a target for terrorism in the first place. Rather than investigate the terrorists' motivation, the government would rather stick its collective fingers in its ears and shout loudly that it's all due to American exceptionalism.

As we all know, anyone that hates America is just jealous of our freedom. A decades-long policy of constant war, occupation, and torture of people in distant lands has nothing to do with it.

(Since the time first addition of this book to the second addition, many of the regulations presented here have already been relaxed as predicted)

CHAPTER 8

Health Care

"Too many good docs are getting out of the business. Too many OB/GYN's aren't able to practice their love with women all across the country."

– George W. Bush

When the American government got involved in health care, costs rose. Basic health care has become incredibly expensive for the average working person not considered poor enough to qualify for government support. Even the free health care offered by Medicare and Medicaid cost more in taxes and inflation, because when the government pays, prices get jacked up. The biggest difference between American health care and that which is offered throughout the rest of the world is the cost of the procedures involved.

There seems to be an assumption that people in countries with universal health care must also pay way more in taxes to cover the costs. The sad truth is that America not only spends more tax money per capita to pay for what incomplete coverage is offered, but that private expenditures on health care (in other words, employer-sponsored health care plans) is now five to six times more than anywhere else in the world. The US citizenry is paying higher health care prices for the privilege of getting less coverage than what can be had in much poorer countries.

America's system is a convoluted one, where for- profit, publicly-traded insurance companies are in charge of covering an individual's health care costs. It's the fair market turned upside-down. Since an insurance company loses money if you get sick or hurt, it's in its best interest to charge healthy people as much as it possibly can, then find excuses to short, if not outright drop, coverage for those who actually need it. It is not as if market forces can properly function when a patient finds themselves in the emergency room. What recourse do they have? Do they have the luxury of choice to say hold on, I'd like to try this other emergency room over here instead?

Instead of shopping around for the cheapest, best provider for the public good, the US government has invested in a system where whoever provides the best kickbacks for government officials, regardless of cost wins. Instead of allowing cheaper generic drugs, customers are forced to buy brand-name. Patents on many drugs are now re-issued, so long as enough insignificant tweaks in the formula have been made to qualify them as "new".

Think about it: why are prescription drugs advertised on TV in the first place? Shouldn't a doctor be deciding what to prescribe you based on your symptoms? The patient should not be encouraged to ask their doctor for a particular drug based on its slick commercial. The bottom line is the bottom line, which is all that matters. It's a business that exists to make money; from the marketer's standpoint, your recovery is simply an optimal outcome, not a requirement.

In 2003, for example, Congress passed a bill called the Medicare Prescription Drug, Improvement and Modernization Act, which prevented the Medicare program from negotiating prices with drug companies in order to lower the cost of drugs. Free market was preempted by corporate favoritism in the guise of government regulation. It is highly likely that Big Pharma wrote the regulation itself. Whether Medicare intended to do its best to negotiate lower prices on behalf of consumers or not, the bill renders such speculation a moot point.

* * *

Before the time when the government got involved in the medical industry, we did not have the need for so many publicly sponsored programs, because what was already available was actually affordable. It didn't cost hundreds or thousands of dollars for a single visit to the hospital; patients could pay their bill out of pocket. No one was tossed out onto the street for inadequate insurance. Young people didn't avoid medical attention for serious injuries or illness because they were afraid of a spike in their health insurance premiums, or worse, because they didn't have health insurance in the first place.

Of course, as of 2014, we all get to pay for health insurance, whether we can afford to or not, thanks to the passage of the Affordable Care Act.

The Affordable Care Act (or "Obamacare" as it is popularly known) is little more than the imposition of an annual, interest-free loan on behalf of the insurance companies, to be later partly compensated by the government when the bill comes due. Despite the government's intent to offer coverage for all by passing the ACA, millions of people still find themselves without.

The problem is, insurance really isn't the way we ought to be doing things in the first place. There are dozens of functional, state-level health care systems that don't rely on insurance companies all around the US, and which the government refuses to copy. Then there's Canada, which is often held up by anti- universal health care advocates as a prime example of just how bad a public system can be. They neglect to mention that a portion of the problem is all the Americans willing to jump across the border to enjoy that free care without paying into the system.

And what about the systems that exist in Taiwan, Japan, France, and so on? There are plenty of working health care systems that could be learned from.

So why does health insurance remain so expensive? It's expensive because of government protectionism. Under the new system, you can't cross state lines to buy insurance, which eliminates open competition. You also can't buy generic drugs, or shop for prescription drugs overseas. And the government still has done nothing to address the core problem: the high cost of procedures.

Everything remains so expensive because of the state. The only reason people on the bottom need the state's help to afford care is because the state made it unaffordable in the first place. It has crippled the concept of universal health care in the same way it has the free market.

We know this because a market system was actually working in the US prior to all the government meddling. But now, the US has neither. We now have the worst health care system in the industrialized world, bar none. Medical bills are the number one cause of debt in the US, even more than housing. People are literally dying or going bankrupt thanks to our health care system. Just imagine if insurance paid for groceries, everyone would buy steaks instead of hamburgers. Prices would skyrocket. The same is true for healthcare.

* * *

It is also interesting to witness the rise in the variety and number of required vaccines from country to country. While vaccinations are a necessary medical advancement and a benefit to society that does not mean that every vaccination that is required (i.e. sold) to the public is done so out of a concern for their health. There is the possibility that some vaccines and shots could be sold more for profit than for the public good.

There is also the problem that even doctors and researchers with the best intentions can screw up. However, with the large financial risks posed by class-action lawsuits, it's safe to assume that the medical industrial complex might consider it better to deny everything that can be and then quietly change the problem product. There was a study that claimed that some of the metals used in vaccines could cause to autism. Scientifically, I don't have a position on this. Politically, however, I think it's safe to say that if this were the case the industry could – and would – cover it up.

History has plenty of accounts of similar, equally horrifying cover-ups. Everything from secret human testing, to the selling of blood known to be infected with HIV, and the secret sterilization of American Indians, has been conducted under the watchful smile of government. The Department of Defense has even used their own soldiers as guinea pigs. A portion of the Senate's report:[41]

III. Findings and conclusions

    A. For at least 50 years, DOD has intentionally exposed military personnel to potentially dangerous substances, often in secret

    B. DOD has repeatedly failed to comply with required ethical standards when using human subjects in military research during war or threat of war

    C. DOD incorrectly claims that since their goal was treatment, the use of investigational drugs in the Persian Gulf War was not research

    J. Army regulations exempt informed consent for volunteers in some types of military research

K. DOD and DVA have repeatedly failed to provide information and medical follow-up to those who participate in military research or are ordered to take investigational drugs

L. The Federal Government has failed to support scientific studies that provide information about the reproductive problems experienced by veterans who were intentionally exposed to potentially dangerous substances

M. The Federal Government has failed to support scientific studies that provide timely information for compensation decisions regarding military personnel who were harmed by various exposures

N. Participation in military research is rarely included in military medical records, making it impossible to support a veteran's claim for service-connected disabilities from military research

O. DOD has demonstrated a pattern of misrepresenting the danger of various military exposures that continues today

The US Public Health Service once infected Guatemalans with STDs for the chance to test out antibiotics.[42] In the Tuskegee experiment, the government knowingly gave 399 African American men syphilis and watched them die. [47] So one shouldn't worry about sounding crazy for questioning the safety of what's in a syringe.

We are never going to have a healthy society as long as sickness remains a profit opportunity, something which doesn't help alleviate people's doubts about the motives behind selling vaccines. It would be an overreaction to reject them all out of hand, for there actually are harmful diseases which can be prevented by vaccination.

The problem is that the for-profit medical industrial complex isn't above exaggerating the seriousness of a disease to incite public fear, just to push a new vaccination or medication that isn't really necessary. After all, the consumer cannot really say no. The knowledge available to the average consumer as to which medicine they should buy is not as comprehensive as, say, the knowledge they need to buy a pair of shoes, so they put their trust in authority figures to advise them in their purchases. This is why a free market solution, absent of an education in these matters, simply cannot work.

Every few years a new scare crops up in the media, be it the West Nile virus, mad cow disease, SARS, bird flu, pig flu, the new pig flu, or the pig flu spelled out with fancy letter-and-number combinations like H1N1. It's shocking how such impressive-sounding threats manage to eclipse the severity of the regular flu, which kills more people per year than all the others combined, and that by several orders of magnitude.[5]

* * *

When it comes to over-prescribing medicine, though, those associated with mental health issues are the clear winner. The largest number of these are those used to treat hyperactive disorders and depression, neither of which has a straightforward, verifiable test for diagnosis. Mental disorders exist and should be treated, but that does not mean every person diagnosed with a chemical imbalance actually has one. And even if they do, there is no guarantee that simply dosing them with pills will make any difference, either.

---

[5] The government has done human testing on everything from how well clothing can protect one from the cold to how well medication works on syphilis. Fun fact: the urban legend that 50% of body heat is lost through the head stems from the misquotation of a military report from this era. What the original report actually said was that, after covering up everything but the head, the majority of heat was lost from that point. Heat loss, however, is a simple math problem of surface area; the most heat a person can lose from their head is about ten percent.

Depression, for instance, can be the perfectly rational response of an intelligent person who has become aware of the incredible level of stupidity pervasive in our society. Gifted young people especially may find themselves intellectually isolated, or worse, ridiculed for their inquisitiveness and critical thinking.

Likewise, a kid who has trouble paying attention in school could very well be inattentive because they are frustrated with being forced to sit and listen to boring, impractical, pseudo-academic indoctrination for hours a day. They are graded not on their comprehension, but their willingness to show obedience and their ability to memorize what they need to produce the proper answers for a test. Two weeks later, they probably won't remember any of it, nor will they have to. Having such an awareness of just how little of their hours spent at school actually count, can't have the best effect on their ability to focus.

I have been both a student and a teacher. I have taught school at all levels, from elementary to college which has given me a good insight into the system as a whole. I believe the only thing wrong with many students is that they've been indoctrinated to believe that their life and future occupation hinges upon their ability to complete meaningless tasks, whether it be a standardized test, or the busy-work that passes as homework nowadays. They live in fear that just one bad day, or one bad test, has the potential to screw up their whole future. That's an extreme level of stress for a young person to have to carry around.

It's even harder on the ones who can recognize that, by and large, they are not being taught enough usable skills to justify the number of hours they are being forced to put in. Before doping up people who react negatively to their environment, why not first check the healthiness of that environment? When around a fourth of the population (and in some age brackets, up to a third), are suffering from some form of depression, maybe it's not the people themselves who are messed up.

Maybe it's the society they live in that needs a change.

One critical issue that needs to be addressed is the drain on the system caused by granting illegal immigrants access to public health care. Left unchecked, such permissiveness may act as beacon to attract even more illegal immigrants willing to take advantage of that system. I support the notion that the process to become a naturalized citizen needs to be made easier and faster, but at the same time, the laws that exist to stop illegal immigration need to be properly enforced. Illegal is illegal. Those laws exist to prevent publicly subsidized exploitation of critical services intended for American citizens. We cannot afford to ignore the issue merely out of the fear that we might be labeled prejudiced.

And while illegal immigration does create problems for health care, it pales in comparison to the overall burden imposed on the general public created by inflated procedure costs, bad regulations and the influence of the insurance and pharmaceutical lobbies on the government. By comparison, the effect of illegal immigrants on the system is an insignificant fraction of the larger problem.

CHAPTER 9

Regulation as Protectionism

"The philosophy of protectionism is a philosophy of war."

– Ludwig von Mises

The US economy is like a sick patient who refuses to take their medicine because it tastes bad. Guys like Peter Schiff, president of Euro Pacific Capital, correctly predicted the threat posed by the housing bubble, and when he tried to warn the public, the establishment hacks just laughed at him. He also warned us about the dangers of quantitative easing (i.e. the Federal Reserve pumping new money into the money supply in the form of interest-bearing loans).

To paraphrase one of his analogies: instead of taking the medicine, they just take a shot of quantitative- easing Novocain, and say with a big grin that the pain is gone. We can only repeat this process a few times before we collapse from the economic equivalent of organ failure, when our creditors get sick of being handed ten stacks of Monopoly money for every stack of real cash.

Pseudo-economists like Paul Krugman reassure the masses with their sincere belief that the best way out of debt is to spend even more money that you don't actually have. Mr. Krugman, for those of you unfamiliar with the man, is someone who so far has been wrong about, well, pretty much everything. Even your average, upstanding pirate radio station hidden in the back of some guy's garage would have too much self-respect to have this man on – unless, perhaps, they were looking for some comic relief. And he's been more than just wrong. This man is the prognostic equivalent of the proverbial umbrella you're supposed to take with you to prevent the rain; for every prediction he has made, the polar opposite is what has actually happened. Yet he continues to make a living by getting invited back to sensationalist economic-propaganda news sites on a routine basis, where he continues to spew his rhetoric.

Murray Rothbard, co-founder of the Ludwig von Mises institute and famous heterodox economist of the Austrian School of Economics, spoke about the origins of progressive regulation.[43] Throughout history, corporations have formed cartels in an attempt to create monopolies in the market, but they have all ultimately failed. Why? The problem with a cartel in the American market is that it takes only one disloyal member to break ranks with the group's attempt to collude on prices or cut production.

In a healthy market, however, such manipulations of price through business mergers, or intentional cuts in production, create an opportunity for newcomers to come in and undercut the established interests. After all, with unsatisfied consumer demand and the actual cost of production being less than the price being set, all they have to do to win is play fairly. Another ironic side-effect of cartel-influenced price inflation is that the market they seek to control becomes more attractive through their own efforts. Inflated prices mean higher perceived profits for new competitors; the sooner they come in and introduce competitive prices, the quicker the cartel is busted.

Another cause for the collapse of a cartel is when betrayal comes from the inside. As the saying goes, once a crook always a crook; an industry insider knows that if he just dropped his prices a little more than the rest of the inner circle he could corner the market on prospective buyers. This particular form of greed-motivated back-stabbing is called secret price- cutting.

The siren call of wanting to have just a little bit more of the pie motivates businesses to break ranks with their cartel compatriots, and use their insider's buyer list to make unsanctioned deals. It's what businesses call a "rate buster" (also known as a "scab" when the equivalent is done to a union). And while it takes a lot more than a single scab to bust a union protest, it only takes one rate buster to undermine a cartel.

So inevitably the cartels turn to the government to enforce their rules. For example, the railroad cartels used the ICC (Interstate Commerce Commission) to outlaw their own particular encounter with secret price-cutting. The clever way they managed to sell this to the layman was by officially pronouncing that it was all done in the public interest. They called for all books to be opened in the name of airing secrets and laying bare what everyone was up to. In reality it was so that each business would be able to keep an eye on his competitors, and make sure they kept trust with each other.

Another lesser-known but still-classic example is what Robert B. Anderson managed to pull off in 1958 Backed by the government, Robert Anderson, Secretary of Treasury under President Eisenhower, led a team to devise a system under which limits were placed on how much low-cost foreign oil each oil company could import into the US. They mandated a quota system, enforced by law, requiring the exploitation of domestic sources of oil as well. Each company was granted a certain number of tickets, which allowed them to purchase a set quantity of foreign oil per ticket allotment.

It might seem obvious that most of the inland oil companies didn't see the practicality of importing foreign oil, instead leaving that to their coastal-region counterparts. As a result, the east-coast corporations were buying huge numbers of tickets from their inland counterparts, which had no use for them. This allowed them to continue buying more foreign oil than ever, with the added benefit of making some money in the spread between the price differentials.

The inland companies essentially became pointless middlemen who sold more tickets than oil because of the new quotas placed upon domestic oil, and the limits placed upon foreign. This ticket allotment scam is a lot like what would be proposed 50 years later in the carbon-credit system created as a weapon in the battle against global warming (in reality, it only managed to mask some massive market manipulation performed in the name of environmentalism).

Nelson Rockefeller managed to give away $900,000 worth of Texas-Louisiana property to Richard B. Anderson, who was himself the president of the inland-based Texas Mid-continent Oil and Gas Association. Standolind, a subsidiary of Standard Oil Co. of Indiana (yet another of the inland companies) also paid Mr. Anderson a $300,000 "finder's fee" to hire a driller for their property. This was like giving money away, as the driller he found turned out to be his good friend, Sid Richardson, whose office was only a block away from Standolind.

As a result, Standolind's parent company, StandardOil Co. of Indiana, made a windfall of about $193,000,000, thanks to the very quota/ticket system that Anderson himself had created. None of this was good for the nation as a whole, least of all for the consumers. It didn't actually reduce the purchases on foreign oil; rather it just forced the east coast, west coast, and Hawaii to buy tickets from the Midwest before they were allowed to import it.

If it makes you feel any better, you might like to know that Richard B. Anderson was sent to jail in 1987, at the age of 76, for tax evasion and money- laundering.[44]

In modern times, regulations are set in such a way that virtually any new business needs a remarkably large amount of capital to get started. Rather than encourage innovation and new business, this system nickels and dimes potential entrepreneurs to death. This allows the major franchises to continue to expand unchecked while newcomers waste years just saving up enough money to risk opening a business, let alone become competitive. There are so many rules in so many industries that one needs a lawyer to understand them all. Sometimes the government seems to make regulations just for the sake of generating revenue through the requirement of licenses, registrations and inspections, regardless of their actual efficacy.

For a more relatable example, let's look at the story of Kris Swanberg, a former public school teacher, who started her own ice-cream making business under the brand "Nice Cream". Unfortunately for her, she chose to do so in the less-than-free market of Chicago, Illinois. After many years of successfully selling her ice cream through outlets like Whole Foods, the IDPH (Illinois Department of Public Health) came to tell her that she would have to change her product. From now on she would have to use a pre-made ice-cream mix, and switch from fresh strawberries to processed strawberry syrup.

In addition, the state informed her that she would have to meet several other requirements. First of all, she would need a dairy license. She would also be required to work out of her own commercial space. She would have to change all of her packaging and labeling to meet state standards. For health reasons, she would have to get her product tested twice a month for bacteria, and was told she would have to buy a pasteurizer (for a mere $40,000) if she wished to continue using organic cream. She protested, telling them that it was her use of organic cream and real fruit that had attracted her customers in the first place, and which set her apart from other ice cream manufacturers. The IDPH didn't care.

The truth is that there was nothing harmful about her ice cream; people had been buying and enjoying it for years. But she wasn't a large enough producer to be able to shrug off such costs easily, and because of the expense the ridiculous regulations in Illinois forced upon her, she probably never will be.

This is why small businesses hate government regulation (to get a humorous whiff of some of the insane regulations all around the United States go watch Why Can't Chuck Get His Business Off the Ground? on the Institute for Justice website).[45]   Let me stress again that this doesn't mean regulations are intrinsically bad; it's simply that many of the regulations we've wound up with are either pointless, state-sponsored leeching, or protectionist policies put in place to protect the interests of the corporations that wrote them.

The practical outcome of regulation is that it ends up working a lot like tax brackets, which have been established to protect the wealth of those at the top. Those below them, taxed out of 35% or more of their incomes, can hardly afford to challenge the upper class's position of affluence and power. This top group then hires clever accountants to ensure they keep their wealth through the use of clever loopholes that allow them to pay fewer, if any, taxes. This protects those who dwell in this rarified atmosphere from any threat posed by the classes below. In the same way, expensive government regulation creates less competition in industry, which in turn allows modern cartels to succeed in a virtually competition-free market.

More often than not, government regulations are to protect established businesses from other businesses, not to protect the consumers' interest, health, the environment, etc. This is why you cannot be knee jerk anti deregulation. Nor should one automatically be anti-regulation. It has to be on a case by case basis. Most of the time however large governments make large regulations for the benefits of large corporation who often are who wrote them.

Just look at the housing bubble. The Fed set interest rates low and the banks began their mortgage-backed securities fraud gambit. After everything fell through, the government came along to bail out the irresponsible parties before finally informing the public that it was their job to foot the bill.

As a result of this mess, the cost of housing nowadays still remains artificially high. The prices never would have never reached this point without all the "easy money and loans for all" policy created by the so-called "risk-free" banks. A truly free market would have never allowed a centralized bank to set interest rates, never removed risk from the lending side of a mortgage, and absolutely never would have bailed out any bank attempting to commit fraud at the taxpayer's expense.

People who saved money for a home because they didn't want the burden of a huge loan were out of luck, thanks to the irresponsible people and greedy banks that had pushed up costs during the credit bubble. Prices were based on hollow promises of credit, not actual capital, and the money for the IOUs simply wasn't there. But instead of letting housing prices fall and the guilty banks fail, the government jumped in to prop it all up. The cost of living, more than anything else, is what straps a person into financial immobility, and assures that their hard work never progresses beyond the hand-to-mouth necessity of paying their monthlies.

The worst injustice of all of this was that no one was held accountable. As far as the public knew, the bubble just happened. Intentional theft was chalked up to bumbling incompetence. The idea of accepting the corporate bailouts as a necessity was pushed onto the public through scare tactics. Simultaneous to the government's public bailout of the finance and car industries was an additional, secret bailout, orchestrated by the Federal Reserve. It left none the wiser, despite the breathtaking scope of its audacity.

In China, there exists a sad, strange situation where families live in overcrowded housing, complete with dirt floors and water shortages, while only a stone's throw away sit modern apartments, empty and unused made unaffordable because the government has allowed speculators, domestic and foreign, to jack up the price of entry in the hope of a high return on their investment. The result is a country dotted with vast, empty cities, complete with all the modern amenities, surrounded in turn by the squalor of polluted, disease- ridden ghettos of the homeless. Despite retaining at least the label of communism, there are disturbing parallels to be drawn between the situations in modern China and the US. Perhaps it would be more accurate to say that China, like the US, is rapidly becoming a plutocracy where only the rich can win.

CHAPTER 10

American Welfare Overseas

"International aid is just another praetorian business enterprise."

– Arundhati Roy

The same system applies to foreign aid. How much do you think a project for infrastructure will cost when the companies involved know that there are millions, if not billions, on tap through foreign aid? Of course the prices are going to get jacked up. Government employees are well aware of this, but rather than fight it, they embrace the revolving door that is the reward for gaming the system. They are all milking the government ATM machine (the only problem being that the withdraws from the ATM machine are not their personal bank account; it's yours and mine).

We have foreign aid used for war profiteering.[46] Paying more doesn't make the military equipment any better, just more expensive. That's the one issue liberals seem to halfway get, but conservatives do not.

I say halfway, because as long as you wave the flag of humanitarianism, even military intervention gets a green light, no matter how ham-fisted the propaganda is. Even then there remains a faction within the Democratic base that is not fooled by this, and remains staunchly anti-war but only if a Republican is in office.

How much of this aid actually even reaches its intended targets? Look at the basic infrastructure in Iraq or central Africa. Just where are these billions of dollars really going? Dr. Ron Paul has pointed this out about foreign aid: "That's when you take away money from poor people in a rich country and give it to rich people in a poor country."[47] If only that were as deep as the crime went.

Foreign aid ought to be thought of as government-to- government bribery. All over the world, despotic regimes are propped up by US aid. The apartheid state of Israel gets the largest amount of aid from the US, despite their policies of open ethnic cleansing, racial segregation, and the demolition of homes. Bahrain, which enjoys a storybook-level dictatorship, is also propped up by the US. Islam Karimov of Uzbekistan, who has openly shot people in the street, boiled them alive, or frozen them to death, also reaps the benefits of US aid.[48]

The monster, Paul Kagame of Rwanda,[49] gets so much foreign aid from the UK and the US that it accounts for 40%[50] of his country's entire budget. Kagame repurposes the funds for the slaughter of people in the Congo, where millions have died. Compounding this problem is the even larger government institution, the UN, which continues to give Rwanda arms, only to see those arms passed off to M23 rebels in the DRC, who murder people for the purpose of securing resources and territory.

Millions have died without a word about it in televised media, not to mention not one discussion about the effects foreign aid might have on the problem. The assumption is this: foreign aid puts food in the mouths of poor people. The reality is that it more often puts bullets in them. A better solution would be to strike at the root of the problem, rather than the symptom.

Many of these countries would not even be as poor as they are were it not for the effects of neocolonialism, and the IMF's own predatory lending. It is not as if whole continents of people can somehow, magically, become poor or incompetent by a coincidence of geography. The truth is more realistic: they do not control their own money supply, and thus have become vassal producers of raw goods for the privileged few.

The problem this time around does not involve the clandestine efforts of a large corporation, but lies wholly within the purview of the government. Certainly, when government and big corporations get together, we tend to have the biggest messes. But the mere existence of Coke and McDonald's in the world is not the biggest factor in why people are starving.

People are starving because they don't have any money. They are in dire straits because of their government's borrowing habits. Their government's employees profit on a personal level, but it doesn't come free. Any subsequent debt or pain is passed on to the common people. Governments, not businesses, are at fault for having borrowed so much money that they make the private individuals' savings useless, and still find time to tax them on top of that. The food and resources aid is meant to provide exist, but the people don't have the financial wherewithal to buy them.

Separate business and state. When a business screws up, at least it can be replaced by a worthy competitor. It at least has the incentive of self-preservation to try to comply with public demand. The worse that can happen is everyone working there loses their job. However, when it is the state that is consuming most of the wealth in internal costs and is doing a lousy job while they're at it, there is little that can be done. After all, it is much harder to replace a government than a company. When states fail, everyone suffers. But they prevent the natural evolution that occurs the market by force.

Aid takes away the agency of an industry. If you are trying to sell shoes, and a government backed, sometimes multi-government back group sets up right next to your shop and gives away shoes, what happens to your shoe store? Of course you go out of business. What happens when there is massive agricultural aid dumped into an area? The farmers and ranchers cannot make a profit and so they seek out new ventures. But then what if the aid stops? Well of course there would be a shortage of food because the market cannot instantly correct itself to create agriculture especially since this is an industry that is often takes entire seasons to make products. A western or Chinese business might not want African lands used for growing food. The humanitarian aid might not be altruistic. Maybe they want to grow rubber on that land instead; much like in early colonial America where the crown forced the colonies to grow tobacco and made them dependent on imports for food. Trading with Indians was a method of escape for this and so it was also in the crown's interest to sour relationships with the natives, or make them impossible. It is extremely hard for African nations to help one another too. For more on that see this film I made.[6] Try opposing humanitarian aid to 3rd world nations and see how popular that will be with the leftist cult of self righteous.

CHAPTER 11

The Environment

"If Al Gore had his way, we would all be recycling toilet paper… all but Al Gore that is" - Scott Dawson

In our society, there are some things everyone agrees are important, such as investing in defense, having a clean environment, and providing a good education to our children. Yet we continue to enable maniacal sociopaths to act with impunity under the guise of the do-gooder lables. It is a scheme of clever self- aggrandizement with a disingenuous theme, intended to protect them from criticism.

Regardless of what you might think about global warming (or climate change, or whatever they're calling it this week), the proposed legislation created to cut carbon dioxide and other greenhouse emissions hasn't actually succeeded. Have a look at Joe Lieberman's 2007 bill, called the Climate Securities Act (S. 2191),[51]   a 548-page bill intended "To direct the Administrator of the Environmental Protection Agency to establish a program to decrease emissions of greenhouse gases, and for other Purposes". Had it passed, it would have not actually lowered emissions at all.

The bill's main purpose was to reduce the emission of greenhouse gasses, but it was also intended to create a federal body capable of regulating a multitude of business industries, from farming to enterprise. Take a look at SEC. 2101-2, which allows people to sell their emission allowances.

Except as otherwise provided in this Act, the lawful holder of an emission allowance may sell, exchange, transfer, submit for compliance in accordance with section 1202, or retire the emission allowance.

And SEC. 2303, which allows third parties to collect interest payment on them!

The privilege of purchasing, holding, selling, exchanging, and retiring emission allowances shall not be restricted to the owners and operators of covered facilities.

It continues: Repayment with Interest: For each borrowed emission allowance submitted in partial satisfaction of the compliance obligation under subsection 1202(a) for a particular calendar year (referred to in this section as the `use year'), the number of emission allowances that the owner or operator is required to submit under section 1202(a) for the year from which the borrowed emission allowance was taken (referred to in this section as the `source year') shall be increased by an amount equal to the product obtained by multiplying--(1) 1.1; and (2) the number of years beginning after the use year and before the source year.

Fortunately for us, the bill failed. What we would have had was a new federal business model where larger agri-businesses could buy up emission allowances from smaller corporations incapable of using them for anything other than reselling. An increase in federal farm subsidies for buyers would just mean we would end up paying for such trades with taxes.

All the bill would have accomplished would be to rope in smaller, formerly independent farms and ranches into a single umbrella corporation. The large farms would lose nothing, as they could afford such expenses through the money they borrow with the capital they receive from the government. Small business will weigh the cost efficiency of production against the short-term gain of just selling their gas allowances to Big Ag. This would ultimately give the larger corporations a greater monopoly over not only production, but the distribution of goods as well.

So the cap-and-trade bill failed, but for the wrong reasons. How many of its supporters do you think actually read it? Virtually none of them. They saw the title, assumed it was pro-environment, and were sold on it without any further investigation. Most of its opponents also never bothered to read it. They just assumed it was anti-business and were sold on opposing it, also without any further investigation. And that is how our congress and interest groups work. No one reads the bills, yet everyone has a strong opinion about them.

I agree with Lieutenant Colonel Karen Kwiatkowski's opinion on the matter:[52] if you need hundreds of pages to describe your bill, then there ought to be an automatic "no" vote. Unless you are intentionally trying to deceive people, then a bill shouldn't be more than a couple of pages long; a dozen at the most. Bills should also be limited to just one subject. It shouldn't be allowed that completely unrelated items get shoved into bills, as they are invariably pork projects, or special conditions added to get certain congressmen to sign them.

* * *

To understand the ugly power government bodies can wield from behind the do-gooder label of environmentalism, one has to look no further than the National Park Service (NPS). America's oldest national park is Yellowstone National Park. From its creation in 1872 up until about 1916, when the National Park Service itself was created, Yellowstone seemed to manage just fine.

By 1934, however, the NPS had to acknowledge that, "It is probable that the white-tailed deer, cougar, lynx wolf, and possibly wolverine and fisher are gone from Yellowstone."[53]   What they failed to say is that the disappearance of these animals was not natural. They also admitted, "In Yosemite the bighorn and grizzly are gone, and cougar almost gone." Once again, this wasn't because of insufficient boundaries, rogue weather, or disease. What had managed to kill the animals so effectively was the National Park Service itself. The NPS had been shooting the animals for decades, despite the fact that it has been illegal to do so since the Lacey Acts of 1894.[54]

They killed the wolves and cougars in an attempt to increase the number of elk. And they succeeded; the elk did increase, into the tens of thousands, and in turn they overgrazed, pushing out the deer and antelope. They cut down the aspens and willows, which in turn affected the beaver, which affected the waterways and so on. There was a cascade of negative results started by the NPS when they began murdering the predatory animals.

Scientific studies have shown that overgrazing, not predators, was the source of the problem. By killing the predators, the NPS had made the problem worse. In the beginning, they hid their activities from the public, but now they are forced to release reports on their "predator controls" (as they call them), but bury them deep in obscure journals kept in the Department of Interior.

From 2007 until today, the NPS has been murdering animals in North Carolina as well, although in this case their activities haven't been restricted to a wildlife preserve, but are taking place in a recreational park meant for the public. The Cape Hatteras National Seashore and Recreational Area was once an area closed to development and preserved for recreation. It's located on Cape Hatteras Island, and the towns adjacent to the park greatly depending on it for tourism. After all, what appeal does an island have without public beach access?

But an activist judge by the name of Terrence Boyle,[7] stayed true to his neo-conservative roots and decided to close down the beach on the island during the spring and summer seasons. The pretext given was the piping plover, a small bird that is not only not actually indigenous to the area, but not even endangered in the first place. The real reason behind the closing was economic: tourism moved away from Cape Hatteras, up the beach to the north side of the Bonner Bridge, where five of the six county commissioners live and do business.

They voted unanimously to give consent to the judge's decree, then fed the public the excuse that they felt that if they hadn't complied, they would have risked the judge deciding to close all of the beaches all year round, rather than just during tourist season. This was either an outright lie or gross incompetence, since no judge, not even a federal one, can overturn constitutional legislation without the support of a legislative body.

The result was the destruction of the island's tourism- based economy, the loss of a vacation spot for families who had been coming to the park for generations, and the theft of a people's land access and cultural way of life. And this tragic list would not be complete without including the most ironic effect of the closure: the measurable decrease in the population of nesting plovers. It turns out that the presence of humans on the beach had been keeping predators away, creating, not destroying, their safe environment.

Of course, it should be noted that, since there were only ever about ten nesting pairs at the population's peak, a loss of even one pair of birds

---

[7] The very same Terrence Boyle who oversaw the Blackwater/Xe counter-suits against the families of men who had been murdered in Iraq. The original suit by the families was to find out the circumstances around the deaths of their sons, who had been burned and hanged from a bridge in a town called Fallujah.

accounted for a whopping 20% of the whole population. As for the NPS, it turns out they can get a bigger budget to police a beach than to provide access to it.

Eventually, pedestrians were conditionally allowed access to the beach, but only after buying permits from the NPS. The presence of people on the beach apparently had no effect on the bird in question as long as the proper fees were paid to the NPS.

This was all a scam to lock down a formerly free, public beach in order to benefit private business, as well as create a new source of revenue for the National Park Service. On the day before the scheduled closing, over 1,500 people used their cars to spelled out the words "PLEASE HELP US!!!" on the beach. Although the gathering was so large that it could be seen from the air, it received no mention in the national media.

In their continued efforts to preserve wildlife, the National Park Service went on to wipe out almost all of the foxes on the island, as they shot them whenever they found them within the park. They also trapped and killed any other animal that happened to walk or fly into the park, including geese, ghost crabs feral cats, raccoons, opossums, and anything else that could possibly kill a bird or harm an egg.

The NPS outlawed all walking and driving on the beach – excluding themselves, of course. This was theft and massacre on a large scale, but it wasn't a foreign army that had taken away the people's land and wiped out its animals; it was their own government. This piping plover scam has already been carried out in other states as well, such as in Sandy Hook, New Jersey. The result was the same: a massive loss of revenue and individual freedom just so the NPS could profit from permits and parking passes.

In December of 2013, the Bonner Bridge that leads to Hatteras Island was shut down. It was public knowledge that the bridge had been in need of replacing for decades, but every time the Department of Transportation (DOT) prepared to start construction, the Southern Environmental Law Center (SELC) would file a lawsuit to prevent the bridge from being built. It appeared that the lifeline for an island where actual people live didn't matter to the SELC. In the end, even environmental lawyers are just lawyers.

Bottom-feeders like Derb Carter, director of the SELC's Chapel Hill office (and life-long bane of Hatteras Island), could care less about environmental impact, economic ruin, or the potential destruction of people's lives, so long as he is guaranteed his $300 thousand-dollar-a-year paycheck. With people like him, if he doesn't have an environmental cause to defend, he will create one.

Derb once even cited environmental concerns as a means to prevent his neighbors from adding a back porch to their house, then turned around and built an even more extravagant one of his own, complete with a walkway that stretches all the way to the water's edge. (This is a bit like the National Park Service's claim that people on a beach disturb birds – that is, until they pay for the appropriate permit, which bestows upon the bearer the magical power of environmental friendliness.)

Now the SELC can't just come out and admit that they don't want any bridge at all to Hatteras without publicly crossing the line of insanity and attracting the attention of the rest of the state and country. Instead, their clever ploy was to suggest the construction of an alternative bridge over a new route Of course, their proposal was for a bridge they knew would never be built, since to do so would mean building a structure 17 miles long, which would have made it the second-longest bridge in the world, and cost billions. Jim Trogdon, who has recently retired as chief operating officer for the North Carolina Department of Transportation, explained to them how ridiculous their proposal was.[55] The more reasonable, two-mile bridge proposed by the DOT had already been approved, with construction ready to begin, when the SELC stopped it.

But to be fair, even the DOT people are far from being the good guys here, even if they are far better than the SELC. The bridge wouldn't need replacing if the DOT itself had not spent years repeatedly dredging sand out from under it just to maintain a channel to the ocean for the millionaires who keep their boats at Pirate's Cove Marina. This has resulted in massive erosion on Hatteras Island, necessitating multiple road replacements and now, finally, the replacement of the bridge itself.

To add to this fiasco, the National Park Service compounds the erosion problem by burning the vegetation that is essential to hold the dunes together, further degrading the integrity of the shoreline. And even the Army Corps of Engineers contributed to the physical and economic destruction of Hatteras Island, when they lugged truckloads of sand to fill in a swamp, all to build a coast guard base which they no longer use.

So who will replace the bridge and build the roads now? Not the government, apparently. The island would have been better off if it had been left to fend for itself. It could have told the SELC to take a hike and kept their road from ever needing replacement by building out the beach, which is currently illegal to do The problem is that, whenever there is an issue involving the environment, there will always be a group of people who automatically side with those they perceive to be protecting nature, because to them every issue is about development versus preservation.

Environmentalism tends to have its own brand of evangelicals who truly put the "mental" in environmentalism. They themselves usually prefer to live in large cities and enjoy easy access to all of the modern luxuries of urban life, but are quick to sacrifice other people's well-being for the sake of their feel-good, pro-environment activism. Even when the reality is that they're unwittingly endorsing the butchering of innocent wild animals and denying regular people their right to enjoy nature.

As if the residents of Hatteras Island have not suffered enough, the government at the behest of a very pushy crowd of pseudo environmentalist, is now building a multi-million dollar bridge over DRY LAND. You read that right. Why? Because it is expensive that is why. The official excuse is because they'd like traffic to pass over top of rather than next to wild life on Pea Island, the land adjacent to Rodanthe, the northern most town of Hatteras Island. Rodanthe is routinely underwater because of the NPS's own policies of burning vegetation and the state government's policy of dredging the inlet. But Rodanthe is full of people. Birds can get protection but people cannot.

This doesn't mean there can't, or shouldn't, be any role for government in managing the environment. The National Parks, under the Department of Interior, were in good condition for the first 40 years, before the NPS, Environmental Protection Agency (EPA), and the Forest Reserve were created under the guise of environmentalism. In reality, they have been used as a clever form of land manipulation while consuming even more tax dollars.

Look at how much just the American government has managed to poison so much of the world so far, with depleted uranium[56] and Agent Orange. Look at how they protect and subsidize Frankenstein projects like GMO foods, or protecting and encouraging the continued practice of fracking into mountain tops with state-arranged trade agreements like the Trans- Pacific Partnership (TPP). Indeed, one must conclude that the government doesn't really give a damn about the environment. If that's the case, then why would you trust them to clean up oil spills or stop pollution, much less manage your parks?

In fact, pollution can be a large source of revenue for the government. In Virginia, for example, the cost in state fines a company like DuPont has to pay for polluting the rivers[57] is less than what it would cost to clean up their act. As a result, every year the rivers get worse, the state government gets richer, and the company saves on the cost of proper waste disposal.

In fact, the largest penalty the EPA has ever imposed was on DuPont, when they fined them $16.5 million for dumping perfluorooctanoic acid (C8) into waterways in Virginia. DuPont had knowingly dumped this waste into the James River. They did it so much that, according to their own documents, they considered decreasing production during times of low river flow. They basically weighed the cost effectiveness of paying the fines for polluting versus the investment costs necessary to stop polluting, and decided it would be cheaper to just pour it in the river

DuPont's labor union began an investigation into PFOA (C8) exposure from their Virginia plant after learning about what had happened in other states. It turns out that DuPont had already been busted for doing the same thing in West Virginia as well, when a town near Parkersburg successfully sued them for $107 million.[58]

The union was disturbed that the EPA had not initiated an investigation on its own. And when you compare the EPA's slap-on-the-wrist fine of $16.5 million to the $107 million worth of actual damage done in just one area, it is clear that the EPA either does not care about, or is ineffective at, curbing deliberate pollution. The state doesn't regulate, it facilitates. As Michael Jackson sang, "All I got to say is that they don't really care about us."[59]

Not even the free market may be able to make corrections for foreign states that do not comply with international laws. Take the super-statist regime of communist China, which ignores practically every environmental and labor law on the books. The resulting cheap labor and cheaper costs of doing business give them an unfair advantage in manufacturing.

The speculation-based economies of the west are only too happy to outsource if it benefits the shareholders, and incidentally getting the benefits, not just of offshore slavery, but of being able to dump inconvenient toxic waste in someone else's back yard thanks to the lax environmental laws the Chinese government provides.

Even those companies which might not want to participate in this brave, new world may be forced to do so just to be able to keep up with their competitors If tariffs were used correctly, they might act as an effective protective barrier to keep manufacturing domestic (or at least in places with humane working conditions).

The problem is that the government would never use tariffs in such a way. When and if they do use tariffs, they are created as selective protectionist policies to benefit businesses with government connections. It is the producers, not the speculators, who should be in the driver's seat of our economy. People need to realize that such entities like the NPS, the EPA, and groups like the SELC really have nothing to do with helping the environment; they're just self-serving crooks with an environmental theme.

Then there are the watermelons. These people are green on the outside and red on the inside. Resentfulness and bitterness are attractive qualities for a communist. Their envy for successful people and wealth and their desire to pull people down, can be dressed up in egalitarian rhetoric. Oh but it's always on behalf of another not themselves. There is something self centered about doing or wanting something for yourself. So it is always good to push for authoritarian change on behalf of another. "Oh this particular thing could be offensive to so and so, we should ban it." Using animals or even better, the planet itself as the other for which to lauder one's own control freak pathology, is a perfect cover. There are some truly self loathing anti-human people out there who just want to cause misery. A commie sees development and capitalism as evil. For if they cannot have something then no one should. Why are so many communist evangelic environmentalists? Because it is another sideways approach to telling other people what they can and can't do.

When explaining this to children, or to Communists, who are usually on the same mental level when it comes to economics, I give the example of school. What if when grades came, everyone just got a 'C' no matter what? No one would fail or excel. Which students would this appeal to? Obviously it appeals to the people making 'D's and 'F's. It would not appeal to people making 'A's and 'B's. Eventually, why even put the effort in to get a 'C' when you are going to get that anyway? Equality of outcome is appealing to losers. Government parks are state owned land, which means no private property. It is very similar to Communism.

Watermelons usually live in cities or at Universities where they can enjoy the fruits of modern life. But they are very willing to tell the state to preserve lands where they don't live, to keep part of the country under developed or worse to keep the third world from using its own resources.

First world watermelons have the audacity to push for stifling legislation on the developing world because they feel that lifting up the living standards of places like India and China would threaten the planet with Noah's Ark style dooms day scenarios.

Their hate for humans is too easy to see through. The world is over populated they say. Having children is selfish. It will destroy the planet. You can see how blindly their self righteous attitude serves to create acceptance for their resentment fueled rage towards happy people and especially families. They don't care about whales or birds; they just need a pretext to be bossy psychopaths, and they need the power of the state to enforce it.

CHAPTER 12

The Mail

"Mail your packages early so the post office can lose them in time for Christmas."

– Johnny Carson

Could the government really screw up the mail? Yes. One might think that, of all things, surely the mail has remained a pure, incorruptible bastion of productive government service. Why, even the inestimable Thomas Jefferson bore the conceit that the government could assume the role of delivering the mail without the eventual – nigh, mandatory! – devolution into dysfunction. After all, the post office, or as it's more formally known, the US Postal Service (USPS), is a wholly independent agency, authorized to carry out its function directly by the Constitution of the United States.

The US, however, does not rely exclusively on the services of such an illustrious organization, but also upon various private parcel companies capable of delivering the documents and packages of individuals the United Parcel Service (UPS) and FedEx being first and foremost among them. However, despite such fair and balanced competition between commerce and state, these disparate entities do not remain entirely separate from each other.

As it turns out, UPS and FedEx report the post office itself as their biggest client. After all, despite harsh scrutiny from the government regarding its ability to stay in the black, it is not as if the post office lacks for business. The problem is, however, that despite constant, daily demands for letter delivery, the post office's almost-guaranteed success has been offset by an artificial employment shortage and draconian health-care cost requirements imposed on it by Congress.

As a result, the post office has been forced to hire out its parcel deliveries to private companies like those previously mentioned in order to keep up with demand. In 2012 alone, UPS and FedEx made almost

$2 billion from services rendered by the post office, while the post office itself reported a net loss of $740 million in the month of August, 2013. This unlikely "failure" was the reason why the USPS was forced to report that, for the third straight quarter in a row, they had failed to turn a profit.

Things have become so desperate that Postmaster General Patrick Donahoe has suggested the idea of expanding the post office's services to include the delivery of beer, wine and spirits [60]   (currently banned under US law), and even the possibility of suspending Saturday deliveries. How is it possible that the post office has become so strapped for cash? There is no lack of demand for their services. But in this, as in many things, it is merely a matter of leaving it up to the government to find a way to screw things up.

In 2006, thanks in large part to Congressman Tom Davis III, Congress passed the ridiculous Postal Accountability and Enhancement Act. Under this act, the post office has been forced to pre-fund their future health care and retirement benefit payments to postal employees for the next 75 years.[61] This means that, in effect, the post office has been forced to pay for people they have not even hired yet.

So just who is taking the USPS's money, and how much? Since reporting losses of over $20 billion, in an act that can only make sense in government, the USPS has been forced to take out a loan from the US Treasury itself. As Ralph Nader, head of the Green Party, has pointed out, had the Postal Accountability and Enhancement Act not been passed, the USPS would now possess a surplus somewhere in the range of $1.5 billion.

By June 2011, the USPS saw a total net deficit of $19.5 billion, $12.7 billion of which was borrowed money from Treasury (leaving just $2.3 billion left until the USPS hits its statutory borrowing limit of $15 billion). This $19.5 billion deficit almost exactly matches the $20.95 billion the USPS made in prepayments to the fund for future retiree health care benefits by June 2011. If the prepayments required under PAEA were never enacted into law, the USPS would not have a net deficiency of nearly $20 billion, but instead would be in the black by at least $1.5 billion.[62]

Esquire journalist Jesse Lichtenstein points out another significant but overlooked fact: "The postal service is not a federal agency. It does not cost taxpayers a dollar. It loses money only because Congress mandates that it do so."[63]

It would seem that we have fallen far from the capable oversight of the first Postmaster General in 1775, Benjamin Franklin, to the current holder of that position, Patrick R. Donahoe. Despite his skill in the execution of his office, and despite the financial crisis created by

Congress, Donahoe manages to take home a base salary of $276,840,[64] making his the second- highest government-paid salary after the president. One wonders how private companies, let alone a government agency, could stand to report quarterly losses in the hundreds of millions while continuing to offer such a generous executive salary with a straight face. However, given time and a certain level of dedicated incompetence, government often finds a way to consume the majority of its revenue in such nebulous administrative costs. *update: The latest postmaster (2018) at the time of the 2nd addition of this book, is Megan J Brennan and her salary was $286,137[65]

For this reason alone, laws and regulations need to be reviewed on an individual basis so that we might see what effects they actually have, rather than what they are purported to do. More often than not, many of them are frequently not only unnecessary, they're outright destructive.

Regardless of party affiliation, one should not be mindlessly cheerleading for or against a particular law based on the ideology of those who support it. People who point to the well-being of the post office as a measure of how a government-run institution can succeed or fail are sorely misinformed. One might think the post office is great because, hey, in general, it does manage to deliver the mail on time. Yet at the same time they may also be unaware of just how deeply in debt it is.

While people often conflate the post office with public schools as an example of how socialist-yet- functional institutions continue to exist in the US, this is one agency that has not been beholden to the purse strings of tax-subsidized government funding since 1970. It is a semi-independent federal   agency, mandated by the Constitution and Congress to be revenue-neutral. Despite this, it remains subject to the insidious attacks of government regulation.

When the government sees a healthy enterprise, they will either tax it or, as in the case of the post office, enact ridiculous pension regulations in order to siphon money away from it in favor of propping up one of the government's many failing enterprises. The government is not a law-making body with the interest of the public at heart; it is the enforcement arm of a select cabal of corporations with whom it has either climbed into bed or been bribed by. Even with functioning systems like the mail, it seems it can't leave well enough alone.

CHAPTER 13

Cops and Drugs

"He who seeks to regulate everything by law is more likely to arouse vices than to reform them. It is best to grant what cannot be abolished, even though it be in itself harmful. How many evils spring from luxury, envy, avarice, drunkenness and the like, yet these are tolerated because they cannot be prevented by legal enactments."

– Baruch Spinoza

Personally I don't advocate the use of illegal drugs, not even something as innocuous as marijuana. But a person has a right to decide what they put into their body, whether it be for medical or recreational reasons. I'm not the only one to have this viewpoint. In the US, two states, Washington and Colorado, have legalized recreational marijuana, (since the writing of this book more have followed) and so far the federal government has chosen to ignore them.[8]

Traditionally, the federal government has long resisted

---

[8] That's not entirely true. The president expressed his displeasure by sending armed men in uniform to assault and rob several marijuana dispensaries in the two states.

legalizing marijuana on a national level, but this time the true value of state-level power won out. Of course it's naturally legal with no state at all. Here is a textbook case where a dedicated group of people worked hard to bring an issue to a state referendum, got the public to vote on it, and passed legislation to support the issue. Voting does matter. Now if only every other issue that goes to referendum would receive the same level of enthusiasm as recreational marijuana has!

Prohibition and taboo have done nothing to reduce drug use; they've just create a profitable black market ripe for violent crime. A market solution, where drugs are legal and open competition exists as a far better solution than allowing the continuation of the condensed, cartel-controlled market, abetted by government agencies that we have now. It would eliminate the huge profits currently made off of illegal drug sales, as well as enable people who need treatment for addiction to be able to seek it legally and safely.

There are many exaggerations about the medical potentials of marijuana. Some go so far as to proclaim it a cure for cancer. But let's not throw the baby out with the bathwater. There are indeed some legitimate medical uses for marijuana. Perhaps the most obvious reason for the use of recreational marijuana – if you ask those using it – is that it is a form of self- medication. People use it simply because they are stressed, or sad, or bored. There is nothing wrong with that. People often indulge in alcohol or tobacco for the same reasons.

Getting drunk is fun. Getting high is fun. And getting high on marijuana is generally considered safer than getting drunk. So why should people care whether or not someone else is smoking pot? Keep your hands off my wallet and your laws off my body. The government has no moral authority at all to put people in cages for using drugs, especially when we consider the number of morally questionable things the government does in our name. If we want to get picky, I might point out that the CIA itself is one of the biggest drug cartels in the world.

The war on drugs has long been a favorite platitude for ambitious politicians trying to garner votes. But just how sincere is the war on drugs? The CIA has been busted for running drugs on multiple occasions. It even created its own infamous air division, Air America, in order to smuggle opium, and was busted for carrying plane-loads of cocaine from Latin America to the US during Iran-Contra.

And the CIA[66] isn't alone; the FBI, Drug Enforcement Agency (DEA), Immigration and Customs Enforcement (ICE),[67] and Bureau of Alcohol, Tobacco and Firearms (ATF)[68] have all been caught smuggling both guns and narcotics under the guise of fighting the war on drugs. The DEA[69] even went so far as to strike a deal with Mexico's notorious Sinaloa drug cartel to facilitate their activities.[70] All of these agencies have been involved with hiring the mafia and protecting drug cartels rather than arresting them.

In 2007, several planes connected to the CIA, including those used in their secret rendition torture program, were discovered to be carrying tons of cocaine onboard.[71] Three different companies – Skyway Aircraft, Donna Blue Aircraft, and World Jet – as well as CIA shell company, Devon Holding, were selling the planes that had been used in the Mayan-Jaguar drug running. The migration of the narcotics was from Latin America to Africa and the US; the cargo sent to Africa then moved to Europe, accounting for about two-thirds of the total sold there. The operation was called Mayan Jaguar, which I've discussed with investigative journalist Bill Conroy, and the investigations are ongoing.[72]

In 2012, yet another CIA rendition plane carrying four tons of cocaine crash-landed in Mexico.[73] As if rendition wasn't bad enough on its own, now we are discovering plane after plane being used to also smuggle drugs. Yet these planes are only the ones we know about, thanks to the crashes. How many more flights and how much more cocaine is being trafficked this way on a regular basis? Author Douglas Valentine has detailed the systematic deception and criminal activities of the CIA, as well as explained how phony the war on drugs is.[74]

Tens of thousands of people have died in Mexico because of the war on drugs; many of them from gunshot wounds. Even though guns are illegal in Mexico, other than for special occupations like the military and police, there are so many shootings each year.[75] So it is very disturbing to find out that the ATF was gun-running high-caliber weapons, not just into Mexico, but directly to the Mexican cartels, under a program called "Fast and Furious". Some US border guards were killed by these same ATF-supplied weapons.[76]

When the program became public, Attorney General Eric Holder's only concern with the subsequent scandal seems to be focused on making the bad PR go away (a common theme with this guy).[77] The excuse that the ATF planned to track the guns is pretty disingenuous, considering the fact that once the guns passed the border they no longer had jurisdiction (not to mention they'd never bothered to informed the Mexican authorities about what was going on in the first place). One would think that not even a US government agency could be so stupid and incompetent. If it turns out they are, then that would be even more frightening than if they had admitted they'd done it on purpose.

* * *

On the more familiar, domestic side of things, law enforcement in America has its own corruption, which goes a lot deeper than just the illegal drug market. The US police force has killed more Americans than all domestic street gangs put together all terrorist attacks since 2001, and even more than the second war in Iraq. They get away with shooting people's dogs, children, and pretty much whoever they want. Worst-case scenario, the worst that happens to them is that they get put on paid leave until things die down; case examples are endless.

For those of you still stuck on the part where I mentioned officers shooting children: no, really. One particularly disturbing case of murder-by-cop was that of Aiyana Jones, a seven-year old girl killed in her sleep when the police performed a no-knock invasion of the wrong house. Officer Joseph Weekly shot her in the neck while she slept on the couch. What made this even more tragic was that the police involved were being followed by a crew from one of A&E's reality TV shows. It's hard to tell if the macho door-ramming and going in guns-ablaze were inspired by the allure of the cameras; in any case, the result was the death of an innocent child. As for the repercussions for the officer who shot her – he was placed on paid leave.[78]

The police can strip, frame, pepper-spray beat up, taser to death,[79] and generally assault people without consequence.[80] They break into houses, search cars without a warrant, run people off the road, steal property, and get paid to do it all. Now technically (not to mention, legally), they're not supposed to do any of these things, yet such atrocities continue. Perhaps it is unsurprising that the police rarely discover any wrong-doing when forced to investigate their own.

The Fullerton Police Department tasered and beat to death one Kelly Thomas, a gentle, mentally ill homeless man, who desperately tried to call out for his dad as he was being murdered by the official representatives of the law.[81] Despite the fact that it was all caught on film, the police were found not guilty of all charges. Not even the charge of excessive force was upheld.

Eric Gardner a father and New York resident was held down and choked to death by several police for the crime of selling cigarettes. He repeatedly said that he couldn't breathe, which means he could barely breathe. Chokes cut off not only oxygen but also blood from reaching the brain. Anyone who has ever done Jujitsu knows that a naked choke can render you unconscious in seconds, and if left applied it will kill you. Even a sloppy one will be lethal. The cop choked him for about a minute. He was murdered on film. Even after he died they were barking orders at his body. All the police were acquitted.

For more on police abuse and the insanity of the American legal system, I recommend listening to my podcasts with Will Grigg on ANCReport.com. You can also follow his work over on his site, Pro Libertate.[82]

Aside from all the trigger happy incidences which are creating a hatred of police in general, there appears to be an enormous degree of theft happing through the process of civil forfeiture. It actually makes sense to look away for a time an allow say a narcotics peddler to generate success, if you can later seize his home vehicles and other assets and incorporate them into your police budget.

CHAPTER 14

Turn Off the Media

"It is advertising and the logic of consumerism that governs the depiction of reality in the mass media."

– Christopher Lasch

Without functional journalism, there can be no functional republic. Without a reliable press, how can people stay informed about the latest financial schemes the government has cooked up, or the truth behind the propaganda of the newest war they're selling? While government waste and corruption are everywhere, nowadays the only real reporting being done is almost exclusively online, and being published by unpaid citizens who feel that if they don't speak out, nobody will.

As an example of just how bad things have become, it's now considered better to watch satirical news shows on Comedy Central to get accurate financial news than to rely on one of the major networks. CNBC airs a long-running show with the un- ironic name, Squawk Box. On this show, grown men (and occasionally the token woman) sit at a long table and scream economic babble at each other. It sounds a lot like a middle school bus with a dozen, deafening conversations going on at the same time. It's not even fair to say that they talk, really; most of the time they just scream-talk, a lot like the children's show character, Dora the Explorer. Perhaps they are afraid that if they talk in a normal voice, they might lose your attention.

Even better is another CNBC show hosted by Jim Cramer. This clown has set himself up with a sound board, and will at times go so far as to cut the heads off of stuffed bears to indicate when he perceives a bull market (not a bear one; get it?)

But it would seem that such anthropomorphic decapitation didn't satisfy him enough, so he decided to extend his bullish/bearish predictions to individual stocks, just for the chance to behead even more stuffed bears. When a program like this counts as the cream of the crop in economic news, no wonder the economy is in such bad shape.

These screaming, prancing jackdaws are just there to encourage the peons into speculating their money away. People from foreign countries who see these shows must assume that they're watching some sort of comedy show like Saturday Night Live, because surely it can't be serious…? And yet, sadly, it is.

One could argue the TV media should raise the standards of their reporting. That would be fantastic, but in reality, such information is out there already in the print media. So instead of waiting for the talking heads to grow up, it might be better if more people would pick up a copy of Forbes or The Economist and read it. If you're into new media, you might also try out some online vloggers such as Jimmy Rogers or Peter Schiff. And don't forget to turn off your TV.

One might think that someone in the media should be tasked to read legislation in progress and report on it to the public. It's bad enough already how the TV news networks serve as the unquestioning mouthpieces of the Pentagon and the plutocrats. When they are not busy reporting outright lies and reading from press kits, they fill up the remaining time mindlessly babbling over celebrity gossip, or the last crumb of scandalous detail from the latest, high- profile court case. The media agencies split their time between deception and distraction.

It's not enough, however, that our current events are being hijacked by infotainment garbage; now it extends to our history as well. It was sad enough to watch the History Channel's slow decent into Jonestown-level, spooky mystery-making, but in 2012, I got to witness it first-hand. One of their myth- making shows featured my twin brother, with whom they had managed to connect with under false pretenses. The show was called The Lost Colony of Roanoke. (The title itself is already misleading, as those early colonies actually went to Croatoan[83] – modern day Cape Hatteras Island – first, then continued to migrate back and forth for years before a portion of the settlers finally went on to Roanoke Island.)

The mystery in question was about what had happened to the people remaining on Roanoke. When the English did not return to the island when promised (due to an unscheduled war with Spain), the colonists simply returned to Hatteras Island, which they had been visiting and living on before they ever went to Roanoke. It is not really a mystery,[84] and for the first 320 years of the island's history never was, until something happened in 1937.

In 1937, Paul Green wrote a fictional play called The Lost Colony. That title alone is what made them lost, not history. There is physical, archeological proof that the colonists returned to Hatteras Island; the primary sources of history we have even now say they went back to Croatoan/Hatteras. But when the History Channel's people arrived, all the host of the show wanted was to create a mystery about some convoluted rock carvings known in the conspiracy world as the "Dare Stones." This kind of conspiratainment is on par with the legends of Big Foot and the Loch Ness Monster. But much like the Loch Ness Monster myth, these stones have long since been revealed as a hoax.

I myself am not the kind of person to categorically reject conspiracies (after all, every covert operation carried out by an intelligence agency is, by definition, a conspiracy). However, this program represented the basest kind of yellow journalism, America Unearthed, received an initial budget of $600,000[85]   showing, if nothing else, that it sure does pay to lie. The worst that came out of all of this is how these myths have robbed the native people of the island of the truth of their already-significant role in American history. What is a worse fate than the death of a people? Killing them and then wiping out their history too.

* * *

As hard as it is for the public to get accurate information about the economy, it should be pointed out that the most ignorant people on the subject are the same ones writing the laws that affect it. In a speech made in Charlottesville, Virginia, Congressman Bob Goodlatte stood in front of a crowd of people who were complaining about inflation and the higher prices on their grocery receipts.

He in turn gave them a condescending smile and told them that inflation is good for savings. How can a functioning adult make such an asinine statement? Mr Goodlatte must subscribe to the same book of nonsense as Paul Krugman, whose best advice to date has to have been that the surest way out of debt is to spend more money.

Ron Paul had the best plan, do away with the income tax and replace it with stop policing the world. Imagine all that money simply stayed in our communities. Giving money to the US federal government is like throwing your money into the fireplace; only the fireplace won't murder or torture anybody with it.

CHAPTER 15

The Banana Republic

"The end of democracy and the defeat of the American Revolution will occur when government falls into the hands of lending institutions and moneyed incorporations."

–Thomas Jefferson

A banana republic is a pejorative term used to describe when the political body of a country exploits the resources and labor of the nation to serve the commercial interests of foreign entities. In return, the political leaders of the exploited nation usually receive bribes or kickbacks. However, in some cases, their obedience may be based on the fear that they will be assassinated or economically isolated, as was the case of the original banana republic Honduras. The banana republic fears being excluded from international capital investment. For whatever reason, be it threat or bribery, the political leadership of that land becomes the puppet of foreign corporations.

In some cases, rather than through the grant of a monopoly on a particular agricultural resource (e.g. bananas, tea, coffee, or sugar), or an energy resource (oil or natural gas), the resulting state-favored monopolies profit through a different method, which is by receiving exclusive deals on construction and infrastructure projects. These firms are then paid far over fair market value through loans, which have been given to the government by other corporations or banks, to build infrastructure such as railways, electrical plants, roads and so on.

This gives companies control over not just the infrastructure they have been hired to build, but also the finances that pay them. As the public incurs the burden of debt for the projects, the companies which made the original loans realize a tidy profit, and the individuals in government who approved the deals receive their promised kickbacks. Essentially, the state and corporate conglomerates work in collusion to create profits for themselves at the expense of the nation's wealth. So much money can be extracted through loan interest, the over-appraisal of project costs, and the monopolization of land use, that it can even influence the value of the nation's currency.

Typically, in response to this type of neocolonialism, a faction of anti-exploitation candidates will claw their way into government and try to nationalize the staple resource that is being unfairly appropriated by the foreign corporations. And as if the battle weren't difficult enough, these corporations may even enjoy the assistance (tacit or otherwise) of the government of their own country. In the case of the United Fruit Company versus most of Central America and the Caribbean, the company had the help of the CIA.

Perhaps not surprisingly, when one finds out that the director of the CIA, Allen Dulles, was on the board of the United Fruit Company. During the Cold War years, if a politician tried to nationalize a resource to protect it from exploitation by private foreign interests, all the US had to do to intervene was point the finger and yell, "Communist!" However, it was, and still often is, America's own fascist policies that push other nations into nationalizing their resources.

In the case of Guatemala, when yelling red did not work for the US, the CIA simply manufactured a scenario to make their case. In 1954,

Allen Dulles's CIA conducted a covert operation against Guatemala called "Operation Washtub".[86] The CIA planted a cache of Soviet weapons on a beach in Nicaragua, then arranged to have them discovered by local fishermen (actually operatives controlled by President Somoza, who was a corporate puppet of the US). Guatemala was the alleged destination of these supposed weapons from the USSR. Just to spice things up, they also threw in a rumor about having spotted Soviet subs off the coast.

None of these things were true. The CIA, through its own outsourced network of subservient clients, had only succeeded in discovering weapons they themselves had planted. Their intent was to convince the US president of a connection between President Jacobo Árbenz of Guatemala and the Soviet Union. At the very least they wanted to give the president a plausible pretext to give the American public in order to justify larger anti-Árbenz operations in Guatemala.

It worked, and Árbenz fell to a CIA-organized coup d'état that same year. It would have been difficult for any corporation, even one the size of the United Fruit Company, to pull off such a stunt without support from the government. It would also have been a pointless task for the CIA to undertake had there not been an opportunity for personal profit through their involvement with the very same companies they were assisting.[9]

The United Fruit Company eventually succumbed to anti-trust laws which forced it to divest and integrate its overseas holdings. Other large businesses under the sphere of big agriculture (AKA "Big Ag"), including former chemical-weapons-maker-turned- farmer, Monsanto, have since arisen to take its place, and with it to employ the same

---

[9] In the age of plastic, many people normally think of energy resources as the monolithic power resource in many nations. For the greater balance of history, however, it has been agricultural products, not oil, which have fulfilled this role.

degree of bullying, legal favoritism, and reliance on state assistance as their predecessor.

In modern times, the North Atlantic Treaty Organization (NATO) and the various intelligence agencies of its member states have worked hand-in- glove with terrorist groups, using states like Saudi Arabia as middlemen to ensure plausible deniability. The Salafis now serve as a convenient pretext for the western military's continued presence, much like yelling communist used to do.[87] It's no longer just about securing the resources; it's about making sure the neocolonial target doesn't. Creating an economic dependency on the western powers is what allows the International Money Fund (IMF) and other international predatory lenders to continue to exploit the third world, as well as prevent any economic or military challenges to the current world order of western hegemony.

CHAPTER 16

The Pentagon's Revolving Door

"The price good men pay for indifference to public affairs is to be ruled by evil men"

– Plato

The US military is the largest umbrella corporation in the world. Although you won't find it on a corporate ranking list like the Forbes 500, our country spends more on defense than all of the rest of the countries in the world put together, and for what?[10]   Paying more for the machines to make war doesn't make them any more powerful, just more expensive. And a comparative analysis of the members of the board of directors for the largest defense contractors, cross-referenced with the parent companies of the major mass media outlets, reveals an alarming degree of overlapping membership. With such an arrangement, it's not surprising that the American public is sold on war like it's a product.

In this way, the modern press serves a PR machine for the Pentagon because they literally own it. Political analysis has sunk to such low levels as to be an insult to the seediest circus, with adults screaming at each other to shut up, call names and trade insults. It's the same kind

---

[10] That spending includes the combined budget of the entire Department of Defense and 13 intelligence agencies.

of cognitive garbage as drives the mindless factions of party tribalism, which can damn an action one minute and praise it the next (at least when the same action is under their banner).

The politicians are being marketed like brands rather than resting on their policies. They issue vague, fill- in-the-blank-with-whatever-is-psychologically- gratifying remarks like, "Yes, we can!" or simple performatives like "change," "hope," and "believe".

They play on demographics. This week a veteran, next week a woman or a black guy; whoever has more media attention will win. The people are choosing among the corporate pre-selected. Monetary policy and foreign policy remain the same, and the only things that change are the celebrity scandals and other non-news sensationalism used to fill up the airtime with nonsense.

The problem is that separating economics from foreign policy is foolish. You can't say, "Well I agree with so-and-so on economics, but not on their foreign policy." These two things are inseparable. Wars are still the most expensive commodity in the world. There is no incentive for the military industrial complex to be cost-efficient. Quite the opposite really; they pile on the pork as much as possible, and then go get no-bid contracts from their cohorts beyond the revolving door.

The Department of Defense (commonly called the DOD, and originally known under the more appropriate title of the War Department) is an unelected arm of government that, unfortunately, gets little mention in the mainstream media's political discourse. While our government-run public education tends to stress focus on the three traditional branches of government and its elected officials, few people are taught much about what is the Department of Defense.

Just to get us all on the same page, here's a brief primer. The DOD has four major sections: the Secretary of Defense for policy, the Secretary of the Navy, the Secretary of the Army and the Secretary of the Air Force. Above them sits the Secretary of Defense and his assistant secretaries.

As of 2013, the DOD Secretary of Defense is Chuck Hagel. Before Hagel, Leon Panetta briefly held the position, and before that there was Robert Gates. He served under both the Bush and Obama administrations, and was involved in the Iran-Contra affair. Before Gates there was Donald Rumsfeld, who returned to the post for the second time, when he helped supply Saddam Hussein with chemical weapons.

Starting with Rumsfeld's Defense Department during the Bush administration, let's take a look at the ensuing revolving-door migration that resulted. As department heads there were Thomas White, Secretary of the Army; Gordon England, Secretary of the Navy; James Roche, Secretary of the Air Force; and Richard "Prince of Darkness" Perle, Defense Policy Secretary (that's his actual, Pentagon nickname).

Thomas White, Secretary of the Army, was involved with Enron as a senior executive. He unloaded 200,000 shares (twelve million dollars' worth) of their stock during that scandal. While White was serving as the vice-chairman of Enron Energy Services, he actively used his political contacts to give Enron a single-bidder contract to privatize the power supply for Forth Hamilton. He was also fond of using military jets for personal trips for himself and his wife.[88]

Gordon England, the Secretary of the Navy, flipped back and forth between General Dynamics and Lockheed Martin. Lockheed Martin is at the top of the list when it comes to Pentagon contracts, and General Dynamics is usually in the top five. England was the president of

General Dynamics' Land Systems Division and later became president of the company's entire Fort Worth division. That division was sold to Lockheed, where he subsequently became the company's president.

Lockheed eventually built the USS Fort Worth, the Navy's third littoral combat ship, [89] and Gordon England was a speaker at its commissioning. After Lockheed, Gordon went back once more to General Dynamics to serve as the executive vice-president of its Combat Systems Group. He left his position in the Department of Defense in January of 2003 and picked up a job in the Department of Homeland Security in the same month.

This didn't last long as England's replacement for the Secretary of the Navy, Colin R. McMillan, committed suicide before he could be sworn in. He apparently decided to shoot himself in the head while awaiting his Senate confirmation. As a result, England returned to become Secretary of the Navy a second time.

In 2005, when Paul Wolfowitz left his position as Deputy Secretary of Defense to become president of the World Bank (a position he won after, or perhaps because of, the brilliant economic failure of his prediction that Iraq's oil revenue would pay for the US military's occupation of that country). Gordon England replaced him as the new Deputy Secretary of Defense. The Secretary of the Air Force at the time was James Roche. He was the president of the aerospace company, Northrop Grumman, which has historically maintained a steady, third-place position behind Lockheed and Boeing as the largest defense contractor. Northrop also employed Paul Wolfowitz, the US Deputy Director of Defense, and Douglas Feith, Under-secretary of Defense for Policy, as consultants, which in reality turns out to be an especially clever way of putting a politician on the company payroll.

James Roche and Richard Perle (Assistant Secretary of Defense and chair of the Defense Policy Board, or DPB), were embroiled in one particular deal involving members of the DPB, Boeing, and Trireme,[90] the private equity firm created by Henry Kissinger and Richard Perle.

The plan was to lease 100 Boeing mid-air refueling tankers to the government under a highly overpriced and totally unnecessary contract worth tens of billions John Warner of the Senate Armed Service Committee would have none of it. The resulting scandal was so outrageous that Boeing had to fire two of its executives, Michael Sears and Darleen Druyun, and then pressure their CEO, Phil Condit, to resign.

But this did not stop James Roche. Even after the scandal broke, Roche continued to push government insiders to go on a propaganda campaign for the Boeing deal. The air force's own studies had already concluded that the refueling tankers were not needed, and would not be needed, for another ten years.

Richard Perle wrote an op-ed promoting Boeing's deal and used 9/11-esque scare tactics as a justification for the sale. Boeing's contract for $23.5 billion was approved by Pete Aldridge Jr. on his last day in office. After refusing to be interviewed by the Inspector General, Aldridge went on to serve on the Board of Directors for Lockheed-Martin.

According to a Wall Street Journal report, Boeing has invested $20 million in Trireme Partners, a firm set up by Perle in the wake of the September 11 attacks and shortly after he was named to the Defense Policy Board. The purpose of the firm is to invest in "homeland security," that is, to profit off the contracts the government has handed out in the so-called war on terrorism. Boeing has also committed

$20 million to Paladin Capital Group, another homeland security investment firm, this one with Defense Policy Board member James

Woolsey as a principal. - World Socialist Web Site [91]

Seymour Hersh, the award winning journalist who broke the stories about the My Lai Massacre in Vietnam[92] and Abu Ghraib in Iraq,[93] dug into the Boeing's connection to Trireme, and soon after Perle resigned from his chair position on the DPB (although he did manage to not leave the Pentagon).

Richard Perle procured Blackwater's first big contract – getting them into Azerbaijan as bodyguards – after that country made a new law that would not allow foreign troops to enter their territory. Blackwater, probably because of all the bad press they had earned, renamed itself Xe, and then after tarnishing that name as well, renamed themselves a second time to Academi.

In any administration, it is commonplace for defense department officials to float between their government loyalties and the corporations they in turn reward with government money. This practice is not just limited to the Department of Defense. All departments do it: the Department of State in particular, followed by the Departments of Justice, Treasury, Interior, Security, Agriculture, Commerce, and, of course, the White House administration for all other conflicts of interest. Perhaps the most immoral among these is the Department of Defense, but then their main occupation is the business of killing.

* * *

The DOD is not above risking the lives of US servicemen, just so long as it will help to increase profits for the military industrial complex. One of the best films available on this subject is The Pentagon Wars.[94]   It makes a case study of the Bradley Fighting Vehicle,[95] with all its useless bells and whistles, and with parts conveniently made in different areas of the United States in order to satisfy the various congressional districts involved in its manufacture.

What started out as a simple transport vehicle suddenly mutated into a semi-aquatic, unarmored tank/scout that could carry far fewer troops than originally proposed. Its cabin walls were made of aluminum, rendering it a death trap. The Pentagon went to great lengths to pass the army's firing test, including filling the gas tanks with water, employing obsolete Romanian ammunition, and hiding the burned remains of manikins that had been placed inside the vehicle in order to test whether or not their clothing would ignite.

Colonel James Burton, the man in charge of testing the Bradley, was fired for his steadfast refusal to rubber-stamp unsafe pork project. He went on wrote a book about the shenanigans he witnessed at the Pentagon during its development.[96] As for the men below him who were responsible for fudging the test results and wasting over $17 billion on a piece of junk that didn't work? They got promotions. It would have better to just use far cheaper Toyota Hilux trucks as the US provided to the FSA terrorist is Syria.

The defense contractor responsible for this death trap was BEA Systems, formerly called United Defense. It manages to hold eighth place among the top defense contractors year over year.[97] Since the first Gulf War at least 50 Bradleys have been destroyed by IEDs[11] and RPG[12] fire. They cost $5 billion each to make and $3 million per year to maintain.

The Pentagon knew how dangerous and useless the BFVs were but made them anyway. After all, the whole purpose of building military hardware, first and foremost, is to generate revenue for the giant corporate welfare queens, and help egotistical peons win fancy ribbons to wear on their breast pockets.

------

[11] IED stands for "Improvised explosive device".
[12] RPG stands for "Rocket-propelled grenade".

* * *

This is not the first time a transport-vehicle-turned- untouchable–cash-cow has proven not only ineffective, but also cost soldiers their lives. Through similar circumstances the US managed to lose 5,086 helicopters in Vietnam.[98] Using conservative numbers on crew sizes and crash survivors, it can be calculated that about 15,000 fatalities in Vietnam were due to helicopter crashes alone. About one-third of those who died were Americans, while the rest were South Vietnamese.

The Vietnamese were able to take down ten or fifteens helicopters at a time, as the vehicle is, by nature, vulnerable to even very basic weapons. On top of that the enemy knew where the helicopter bases were and the routes of their planned flight paths All they had to do was attack a village and the closest base would respond by sending out its helicopters.

The Vietnamese would lie in wait on the ground, and when the helicopters approached, fire an assortment of projectiles including club-like arrows, ropes, and vines to litter the sky.

These would then catch in the helicopter's rotor blades, causing them to crash. To this day, the jungles of Vietnam are peppered with the husks of crashed helicopters, which dot the landscape like an avionic graveyard. Each one represents the loss of human lives. Each one also represents a paycheck to the Bell Aircraft Corporation, the Texas-based company that built the "Huey", the most widely used helicopter in the war.

In 1960, Bell was acquired by the Textron Corporation, which in turn was financed by the First National Bank of Boston. Orders for Bell's helicopters exceeded $600 million (well over $3 billion in modern currency). Perhaps worst of all is that a full 47% of the helicopter crashes were not due to hostile forces; the machines were quite good at crashing on their own, having an average survival rate of only 154 days.

At any given time many of the choppers were not operational, as they required regular, heavy maintenance. Such maintenance required ground crews in the combat zones, which put even more lives at risk and added more financial overhead. But the military brass is not always so much interested in the efficacy or safety of the equipment as they are in who will profit from its manufacture.

The Vietnam War didn't even have the grand strategy or defined goal that the US armed forces needed to win. They were fighting an abstraction called communism, and an uprising largely of their own creation.

Had the American government not taken 1.1 million North Vietnamese captive, ferried them down to the southernmost part of the country and then abandoned them to fend for themselves, we probably would not have encountered the level of widespread violence we did (and therefore no pretext for a war).

If the Office of Policy Coordination (OPC) and CIA cannot find enemies to battle, they will create them. Likewise when the military industrial complex (MIC) cannot profit from peace, it will seek to create conflict, human lives be damned.

Before the end of his term, President Eisenhower had grown disillusioned with what he labeled the "military industrial complex". He introduced this epithet in his farewell address to serve as a warning to the nation, and history has proven him right. He succeeded in leaving office with a surplus as a result of his determination to not to allow another major military contract to be awarded before he left office. He was quite disgusted with the whole process after he saw what a monster WWII and the Korean War had created in the war-related industries. He feared these industries would not accept the inevitable downsizing that comes with peace.

As a consequence, JFK was left with a four-billion dollar air force budget that he could funnel into MIC contracts (specifically General Dynamics), create jobs and thereby secure the necessary votes in certain closed districts that he would need to win a second term. Before the Vietnam War was escalated, the Kennedy administration had already been plotting on how to use the war budget to their political advantage Kennedy's Defense Secretary, Robert McNamara, finagled a way to combine this budget with the navy's, bringing the total to 6.5 billion.

Kennedy had barely managed to defeat Nixon in the 1960 presidential race, with only 112,827 (0.17%) of the popular vote. That gave him a victory of 303 to 219 in the Electoral College. It was the closest presidential election America had seen since 1916. McNamara wanted Kennedy to have a second term, not to mention himself. Goldberg had an office with maps of the country plastered across the walls, color-coded to show which congressional districts had gone to JFK, and which had gone to Nixon. Obviously, 0.17% of the popular vote was too close for comfort.

McNamara, together with Arthur Goldberg, JFK's labor secretary, hatched a plan to use the budget surplus to benefit Kennedy. They used the Department of Labor's statistics to map out proposals for the new TFX fighter jet, which would then become the beneficiary of the surplus that Eisenhower had left to the Kennedy administration.

They mapped out each contract and subcontract by zeroing in on the areas that would be involved. They noted how many jobs they could create in key districts and how much construction would be needed It didn't matter to them whether or not the manufacture of disparate parts could be consolidated in the same place, rather than spread across different states. The contest was eventually narrowed down to two competitors, Boeing and General Dynamics/Grumman.

Most thought that Boeing was a shoe-in; by any measure, they had the better plane. On top of that, General Dynamics was in trouble. According to Richard Austin Smith of Fortune Magazine, General Dynamics had already lost $170 million prior to 1961. They desperately needed the TXF contract.

General Dynamics had done well in the 50's. Their president, Frank Pace, had been the Army Secretary from 1950 to 1953. They also had a friend in Fred Korth, the Secretary of the Navy, who was also the former president of Continental Bank, which had loaned General Dynamics considerable sums. They still had Roswell Gilpatrick, a New York banker who became the Deputy Secretary of Defense in 1962, and the chief counsel for General Dynamics before that.

It was Gilpatrick who made a speech at a banker's convention explaining the rationale for the decision to choose General Dynamics. He said they wanted to make an effort to create work in depressed areas (in other words, areas that had previously voted for Nixon). Alfred W. Blackburn, who worked in the Bureau of Research and Engineering and was a longtime friend of McNamara, resigned over the decision to award General Dynamics the TFX contract. He knew that the TFX contract had nothing to do with national security or combat capacity.

Although General Dynamic's design was inferior to Boeing's, at least the plane flew and functioned – or at least half of them did. In 1968, of the six that were sent to Vietnam only three returned. These were the three that had not crashed due to structural failures. Like the Bradley, the TFX was encumbered with the expectation of serving more than a single purpose. The US Air Force wanted a low-level strike aircraft.

The US Navy needed a long-range, carrier-borne interceptor. They got neither. And the only reason such a convoluted combo-plane was built in the first place was so that McNamara could justify lumping the air force and naval budgets in together on a "general-purpose" aircraft.

Over the years, General Dynamics went way over budget to make further modifications to the plane. Eventually they got something working by basically throwing away the navy's specs and making the plane the air force had requested. Military equipment is sometimes created for the sake of playing regional politics. This was the case in the Goldberg- McNamara plan. In modern times, when fighter jets are not even necessary anymore, the contracts are made simply to funnel money into the weapons industries, so that everyone in the revolving door can continue to profit.

* * *

What could be worse than a hybrid vehicle that combines the worst aspects of the Bradley and a helicopter made by Bell? Let's take a look at the Osprey V-22. Hybrid vehicles of all kinds continue to be made, but today it is Bell-Boeing that makes the V-22 Osprey, an amalgam of helicopter and jet[99]   that manages to distinguish itself through its innate ability to crash.[100]   Often.[101]

 Perhaps Boeing is satisfied that it can brag about making the first helicopter that can land upside- down,[102]   as one Osprey did when it crashed in Florida in 2012. Perhaps that explains why, mere months after the Florida crash, the US sent a dozen of them to its bases in Japan (I spoke about this in an interview for Russia Today).[103]
There were massive protests by the people of Okinawa, but they were ignored. Only foreign media bothered to cover it. Bell-Boeing didn't care, because at $70 million per unit, they were laughing all the way to the bank.

Today, Lockheed-Martin's most modern weapons of war, the F-22 Raptor and the F-35, have huge problems and huge price tags. Investigative journalist Dina Rasor has reported in detail just how wrong these machines are in her piece, "Pilots as Lab Rats: The Reprehensible Risk-Taking on the F-22 Raptor".[104] She explains in detail how both the F-22 and the F-18 despite over-convoluted oxygen systems still left pilots getting sick and passing out. One pilot crashed and died while two more pilots, Captain Josh Wilson and Major Jeremy Wilson, refused to fly the planes any longer and took their story to CBS's 60 Minutes.

Bottled oxygen, tried and true, has been in use in aircraft since 1913. But Lockheed had another idea: why be practical when you can be expensive instead? After all, the government's paying for it, so the more it costs, the better it is for us.

Dina Rasor explained that the F-22 uses an onboard oxygen-generating system (OBOGS):[105] Compressed air from the compressor stage of the jet engine uses a molecular sieve to extract nitrogen, thus increasing the oxygen percentage of the breathing air it sends up to the pilot's mask. Two molecular sieves are needed so they can provide the oxygen while the other cleans itself – a complicated way to get vital oxygen to the brains of the pilots.

She compared it to getting air from your car engine: It does seem odd to take breathing air from the jet engine, a source that could include dangerous contaminants like carbon monoxide or unburnt fuel if the engine had problems, to be fed into the lungs of pilots. It would be like having your car's fresh air taken from the carburetor in the hopes that the fuel mixture would not leach into the air you're breathing.

But that wasn't even the entirety of the problem. Pilots of the F-18 had had similar problems, but nowhere near as frequently as the F-22 pilots. Even some of the ground crew for the F-22 got sick without even utilizing the OBOGS. How could the ground crew be affected? And just what is the difference between the F-22 and the F-18? Both aircraft have the insane, extract-air-from-engine-intake method of making oxygen. One thing the F-22 has that the F-18 does not, however, is a special stealth coating.

It turns out that the laminate coating used to help the plane go stealth is so fragile that it must be recoated every time the F-22 flies through even the slightest rain or dust, helping it set a new record for required routine maintenance. Worse still, it turns out that the adhesives used to hold the stealth coating together also happened to be toxic. When ground crews got sick from these coatings, the government would not allow the doctors treating them to know what the composites consisted of, due to their top-secret nature. One F-22 sells for $425 million; that's nearly a billion dollars to build two fighter jets, whose most cutting-edge capability seems to be making their pilots pass out.[13]

 Worst of all, the special stealth goop that represents the biggest flaw of the F-22 doesn't actually work under real-world combat conditions. It can be defeated by old-fashioned, long-wave radar. Stealth-proof coatings and stealth-proof shapes are a myth. They are only proof to short-wave radar, and then only some of the time.

In 2017 Lockheed got 32.5 Billion dollars from the US tax payers. Let that sink in. This is nearly as much as what the government allocates to the State Department. It is well more than what many other federal agencies get. Lockheed is the new East India Tea company. It is so big it might as well be a state. This corporation also benefits from the foreign aid to states like Israel which is where it jointly built its most expensive project to date the F-35 which has costs more than 1.5 Trillion dollars[106] to produce. The fighter jet doesn't even work as well

---

[13] The F-35, the latest stealth aircraft, has similar issues. Its arresting hooks cannot catch onto an aircraft carrier's standard landing cables, rendering it incapable of a sea landing.

as previous jets. There are a long list[107] of problems with it. F-35b Fuel Tank redesign, problems with : Software delays, lightening protection, flight control problems, helmet display issues, avionics processors, thermal management systems, ejection seat assemblies, cockpit display electronics unit, seat survival kits, igniter-spark in the turbine engines, and even the on-board oxygen generating systems.

 The oxygen problems the pentagon reported as (*"pilot physiological events,"*) There are problems with the tires, landing gear, in fact it the tailhook is not even compatible with US carriers.[108] The Automatic Logistics Information System or **ALIS** doesn't work. The F-35 has also been grounded for electrical problems. You could not find a more creative way to waste $1,500,000,000,000 and counting. This doesn't even include the cost per unit, or maintenance, that's just the production cost. Oh and the stealth doesn't work… on a stealth fighter jet. The stealth coating has even been found peeling off[109] and the repair crews have been hospitalized from dealing with it. They were not allowed to tell the medics what it was made out of because of the secrecy. One thing it can do is something it is not supposed to do and that is spy on our allies.[110] Are these problems just hiccups from the past that have been straightened out? No. In Jan of 2018 the pentagon reported[111] that half of the F-35 fleet was grounded for tech problems! The F-35 is nothing but a Bradley with wings.

Lockheed Martin, if you remember is who gave the seed money to the Weekly Standard which was the Neocon rag which pushed the lies about Iraq the most ferociously in order to offer a pretext for the 2003 invasion. William Kristol and Robert Kagan get the credit/blame for founding PNAC's mouthpiece. However the funding for this Hasbara center piece of Zionist war propaganda was Lockheed Martin. Richard Cummings wrote in Lockheed Stock and two Smoking Barrels[112] how Bruce Jackson the VP of strategy and Planing for Lockheed, gave Bill Kristol the money. It should not surprise anyone that Bruce

Jackson would finance PNAC's media arm, when Jackson was the Executive Director for PNAC. Bruce is currently the President of the Project on Transitional Democracies. PTD has been meddling in Ukraine, and imagine my lack of shock at who comes to defend them.[113] The best reporting on the Ukraine[114] debacle was probably from Robert Perry of Consortium News, unfortunately he passed away this year. Jackson, even though he admitted that he didn't know anything about Iraq was selected to be chairmen for the Committee for the Liberation of Iraq. Since he didn't know anything and was just taking a salary he deferred the actual decisions over to Randy Scheunemann. Scheunemann was on the board of directors of PNAC and the treasurer of PTD. See a pattern there? Dick Cheney's wife was on the Board of Lockheed. They signed up advisors to the board for the Committee for the Liberation of Iraq, such as Richard Perle and James Woolsey. Perle has too many lies to list and Woolsey was the Weekly Standard's source for the lies about Anthrax which wrongly attributed a connection between 9/11 hijackers and Iraq. There was more news about the non existent meeting in Prague between Al Qaeda and Iraq than the actual Al Qaeda summit in Malaysia where the CIA observed future hijackers meeting with KSM. They then openly moved to and lived in the US without the CIA informing the FBI. More on that[115]

Is the public up in arms about Lockheed literally being up in arms? Not really because the news rarely if ever breaks the print media barrier. Televised news is simply too tied up with industry to rattle the cages. It is very hard for them to have a story approved about the MIC or Big Pharma the two pillars of corporate news sponsorship.

Defense may be good, but it is still a business. The military itself is a business. Normally a business will target high-quality goods at a low price, because he who insists on making crap products will eventually go under. However, when the buyer is the government the reverse happens: prices rise, quality ceases to matter, and with just one contract, a single company can outdo its competitors. Our military hardware has gotten so bad that other countries will not even buy it without the subsidy that is US foreign aid.

It's not just the military behaving this way. All of our government's various departments have devolved into for-profit businesses. Alongside the military industrial complex we now have the medical industrial complex, the security complex, the prison complex, and the war on drugs. There are also appalling amounts of money and resources being wasted in the departments of energy, agriculture and education. You name it; they waste it.

When is the pentagon going to create glow in the dark camouflage? After all it seems like it would cost more and be completely useless in battle. Nothing would surprise me. In 2018, after all the problems with the (Bradley with wings) F-35 and F-22, the geniuses in DC announce a new project for Lockheed Martin. They are going to create a Hybrid aircraft out of the F-22 and the F-35. I think the tentative name should be the F-U tax payer. But for now they are going with the F-3. Should this disaster actually be built, it would have a hard time passing the US Air Force's Penetrating Counter Air requirements.[116] You can't make this stuff up.

CHAPTER 17

But in Europe...

"There are two kinds of Europeans: The smart ones, and those who stayed behind."

– H. L. Mencken

But doesn't domestic welfare work in Europe? Many progressives tend also to be Europhiles. There are certainly things Americans could learn from the systems of other nations, but not just in European countries. It is important to remember that a simple political change will not always manifest the same way in a different area, as different places have different cultures, and what works in one may not work in another.

That being said, a lot of arguments by progressives begin with the phrase "But in Europe they do X." Guess what? In many of the places held up as role models by such romantics, the people there are either broke, or going broke. They ran high-tax nanny states for so long that the inevitable result was collapse.

Rather than providing an environment of opportunity based on merit in order to attract hard-working, productive people, such nanny states only managed to drive them away and attracted free-loaders instead. The US hit at an all-time high in 2008 for unemployment and food stamp distribution. But then again, why work at a low-end job with no benefits, low wages and even less satisfaction, when you can just make the same amount collecting unemployment? As I've said before, nothing is more expensive than free stuff.

If we could reach out to the average lefty regarding the ills caused by government intervention, and talk to conservatives about how war only serves to benefit the corporate welfare state, then perhaps we could achieve a real coalition for liberty.

Instead, we get attacked from both sides. The left screams ignorant slogans against corporatism, while the right screams about fears of isolationism. The reality lies in a third direction, and that is that the most conducive route to peace is through trade. The left and right remain subservient to a common emotion: fear. Fear of helplessness, fear of foreign invasion, fear of poverty.

The one saving grace of Europe, and especially Germany, is that unlike the US they are not engaged in a high level of militarist actions around the world, if at all. Sure, France and the UK support proxy wars and will, with NATO support, gang up on much poorer nations from time to time; however, even on a bad day, none of this compares to what the US spends on maintaining its military engagements. The US out-spends all of Europe combined, and that many times over, when it comes to such spending. Given their high levels of investment in domestic welfare, were any of them to decide to mimic the US's behavior, their economy would collapse within a year.

Given the choice, I would prefer the nanny state to militarism, but why not just say no to both? I prefer universal healthcare to the United State's oligopic sick-care system, too, but again, why not refuse both? A thing is not made better just because you can compare it to something worse.

Much of Europe also has no minimum wage laws (including Germany,

Switzerland, Austria, Norway, Finland Sweden, i.e. the countries with the best economic conditions). And yet the same people so eager to copy Europe's domestic welfare programs never seem to say that we, too, might benefit by eliminating minimum wage.

They aren't really looking at European states to discover a more functional political model; they are starting from a personal ideology and then seeking out places to cherry-pick those things that seem to support their own view. The reverse also holds true. People who want to get rid of minimum wage usually fail to mention that those places which don't have it also have a different social welfare structure, universal healthcare and so on.

It is crass to ignore one country's cultural differences while lauding their economic or political systems, not to mention different approaches to diplomacy, availability of natural resources, educational system, etc., as factors for why one state differs from another. Comparisons can and should be made, but not in a bubble. What works in one area might be different in another based on a totally different political climate.

For example, Japan is a nation of savers, almost to the point of paranoia. Their money supply suffers from too much capital being neutralized in rainy-day lockboxes, and so the base suffers from the lack of a healthy circulation of money. The US, on the other hand, also suffers from a depleted money supply for the opposite reasons. People save too little or not at all while running up massive credit card debts.

Credit becomes tightened, and banks and the upper class siphon the actual money supply away from the base through debt collection and interest. Japan and the US need different solutions for the same problem – solving the lower and middle class's lack of access to enough debt-free capital to make the market work. We have to think deeper about economic systems and not allow "fashion politics" to continue to decree wishful solutions of immolation, which start with conclusions and then work backwards to try to prove their validity.

Migration problems in Europe may be the downfall of their social welfare programs. The fear of being labeled prejudice towards race, religion, or ethnic group is preventing opposition to a very dangerous economic policy, namely redistributing wealth to an incoming third world population which continues to take more than it produces. Economically, this system is unsustainable and they will either run out of money or will have to dramatically lower their living standards or both. Protecting cultural integrity is important. For cultures aren't simply trivial things like cuisine and musical tastes. Everything from economic models, work ethic and parenting are imbued in the society by its culture. And some are not just <u>different</u> than others, they are <u>better</u> than others.

CHAPTER 18

War™

"There is no instance of a nation benefiting from prolonged warfare."

– Sun Tzu

Over the last decade, America has engaged in a constant campaign of war and occupation on multiple fronts. So just how are they all working out? That depends on your perspective. If one assumes that the aim of war is to win, then they're going very badly. Winning for us has not even been defined.

If you look at war for what it really is rather than what it pretends to be, then things are going exactly as planned. The purpose of a protracted war is to prolong the conflict for as long as possible in order to procure profit. The more internal struggles that can be can foster the better. The Project for the New American Century (PNAC) stated this openly, as did its predecessor, Oded Yinon. In 1982 he wrote:

Iraq, rich in oil on the one hand and internally torn on the other, is guaranteed as a candidate for Israel's targets. Its dissolution is even more important for us than that of Syria. Iraq is stronger than Syria. In the short run it is Iraqi power which constitutes the greatest threat to Israel. An Iraqi-Iranian war will tear Iraq apart and cause its downfall at home even before it is able to organize a struggle on a wide front against us. Every kind of inter-Arab confrontation will assist us in the short run and will shorten the way to the more important aim of breaking up Iraq into denominations as in Syria and in Lebanon. In Iraq, a division into provinces along ethnic/religious lines as in Syria during Ottoman times is possible. So, three (or more) states will exist around the three major cities: Basra, Baghdad and Mosul, and Shi'ite areas in the south will separate from the Sunni and Kurdish north. It is possible that the present Iranian-Iraqi confrontation will deepen this polarization.[117]

Perpetual, low-level combat justifies a continued US presence and allows for clandestine activities like the liberation of heroin.[118] Religious wars attract in-fighting among local forces like fly paper does flies. This is good for business, and prevents countries embroiled in such conflict from ever rising high enough to become economic or military rivals to the US hegemony.

The war industry is worse than the financial industry when it comes to conspiring to commit criminal activity. Don't think for a second that the intelligence agencies are above lying to the public, or that the mass media would hesitate to cover for them in much the same way they covered for the investment banks with their mantra, "too big to fail."

Governments lie, they steal, they spy on their own citizens, and they murder without compunction. This is a historical fact. The NSA spies on Americans, but only to protect them from the terrorists we ourselves have created through US foreign policy. The thought-terminating cliché that if you have done nothing wrong in your life, then you have nothing to worry about, is bizarrely illogical. What people need to understand is that the real purpose of the NSA's domestic spying is to gather dirt on political dissidents, not terrorists.

With the NSA spying on everyone and the government attacking whistle blowers, how is the public supposed to be informed? How can we hope to change things once all the politicians are bought or blackmailed? The courts are not going to rule domestic spying as unconstitutional, because the very people who select the judges are controlled by those doing the spying. The age of Big Brother has truly arrived.

* * *

So many Americans are now dependent on government just to get food. The nation is at a record high for people on food stamps. Many industries were also hurt by the housing bubble – construction in particular – and when that ended, so did all the jobs related to it. It's not as if the country is lacking in skill and talent; it's lacking in capital. There is no money to pay the workforce. People have to understand how much the quantity of money in circulation effects everything across the board.

The youth especially have been hit very hard. Colleges are too expensive and housing costs too high because of bad government taxes and regulations. The jobs needed to afford these higher costs of living aren't there, thanks in part to government regulations and taxes. Healthcare is unaffordable. These young people are forced to pay into social security, even though in all likelihood it will not be there for them in the future.

It is no wonder that those who can are leaving the US. Others are joining the military as a form of employment, and a way to avoid months or even years of fruitless job-hunting in the real world. Others become professional students, finding it easier to stay in school and avoid the abysmal job market altogether

A functional government ought to be issuing money to serve the public interest, protecting individual rights, and promoting economic freedom to encourage the productivity of individuals. Instead they allow the money supply to contract at the will of a private corporation, which then loans the money out at interest. As Thomas Aquinas said, "You can't lend out that which is consumed in its use."

In other words, collecting all the money you loan out plus interest means you are trying to collect more than what was actually created. The end result is that the money owed is greater than that what actually exists in the money supply, thus making it impossible to ever pay the loan back in full. All the problems outlined in this book, from military waste to corporate bailouts and fraud, could be fixed or at least greatly reduced by one simple act. The government needs to stop borrowing money.

It's bad enough to create money out of thin air, but it is even more stupid to let someone else do it for you and then lend it out with interest payments. We could at the very least kill the middleman. Monetary reform should be the meta-issue that all Americans should be concerned with first and foremost. In fact, considering the balance of wealth in the current global economy, it should be the meta-issue for everyone everywhere.

Thomas Edison once wrote, "If our nation can issue a dollar bond, it can issue a dollar bill. It is absurd to say our country can issue $30 million in bonds and not $30 million in currency. Both are promises to pay but one promises to fatten the usurers and the other helps the people." The problem is, with all the distraction media and general disconnect from the political process, no one in America is utilizing the system their forefathers fought so hard to create.

Protesters spend a lot of time marching around in parks, playing drums and waving signs, but how many of them actually set up meetings with their representatives, as is their legal right? Some go online to rant endlessly about politics, but how many times have they written a physical letter to a person in government? If this inspires you then perhaps you should do it right now. Write a letter. Pick up the phone. If I can motivate even a few of you, dear readers, it will be worth it. Go ahead, I'll wait.

Today's American activism is directionless. Worse yet, there are many people who support our nation's wars but are unaware of their disastrous effects on the economy and on trade, and who are also clueless about monetary policy. It is our culture that has raised these people to think this way. And with the media functioning as a propaganda machine for the Pentagon, and schools indoctrinating our young people with "USA, love it or leave it, we're the bestest country on earth!" How can the United States hope to kick its addiction to war? And if it doesn't, will the inevitable result be its economic collapse?

If we truly care about justice then we cannot allow these wars for profit to continue. We cannot continue allowing the government to murder in our name. We cannot continue to allow the press to manipulate our youth into unconditional loyalty to militarism, or confusing what it means to fight for freedom from tyranny, rather than fighting for what the government wants.

We desperately need a cultural shift away from an ingrained reverence for soldiers and instead take a hard look on a case-by-case basis at all of the government's imperialistic escapades. We shouldn't allow the warhawks to accuse people of not supporting "our boys" when the actual issue is that we don't support their pointless wars. It's not opposition to the troops; its opposition to sending the troops into needless conflicts and putting their lives in jeopardy over nothing.

In the December 2013 hearing on Afghanistan, no one on the panel could answer how much the war was costing us per year.[119] No one on the panel could say how many Americans had died, either. They didn't know because they didn't care. All they knew was that they wanted it to continue for another five years.

* * *

If you live in the United States, all you have to do is open a history book, or turn on the TV, and it will be filled to the brim with war. War is the most vicious act mankind can inflict upon itself and yet the fighting is wrapped up in stories of glory, nobility and honor, and always given the air of righteous necessity At best it is a necessary evil.

The American people are consumed by war. Some pour over Civil War or World War II books, memorizing every bit of minutia involving tactics and strategies and playing "what if" games. There are countless movies about war, focused squarely on the actual fighting and told from the perspective of the victors.

The true horror of war and the perspective of the victims seems to get glossed over, hardly warranting a footnote in the narrative. The one exception would be the Holocaust, in the so-called "good war", although one might think it appropriate to document the equally horrid butchering of millions perpetrated by the allied side as well.

The grim reality of war is that the majority of deaths nearly always come from starvation and disease, with the principle victims being civilians who want no part in the conflict. There is nothing glorious about a bunch of mostly poor young people being deceive by the state into risking their lives to murder the downtrodden of another region, all so some corporate interest can thrive off of the bloodshed.

In history, war has usually involved one set of poor people fighting with another all for the sake of furthering the ruling class's own selfish goals. It has almost always been based on lies. Currently, in the US, we are experiencing an overwhelming degree of rhetoric about American exceptionalism. Any paper- thin deception serves as a justification for war. And yet, even when that justification is proven false after the fact, there are no consequences for the instigators. The war party (usually being whichever one is currently in power) simply changes its rationalization by propping up its latest thinly veiled pretext.

One of the most common tactics is to invoke World War II (commonly referred to as "the good war") and create new Hitlers to justify a new wave of military adventurism. The war propagandists always blame American isolationism for the incredible scope of WWII, rather than Hitler's blatant militarism, as if it was something that just came out of the blue.

The roots of WWII can be found in the Allied's treatment of Germany post-WWI, which is enshrined in the Treaty of Versailles. Violence begets violence. In this case, it was the gutting of a country's resources, the theft of land, and the starvation of its people brought about by the impossible reparations demanded.

Some warhawks have even gone as far as to say WWII ended the depression. This is a horribly crass generalization, only made possible by a complete ignorance of economics. But such ignorance and the industry of war help to obfuscate the more sinister facts behind why and how wars get started and promoted.

Over time, warfare has become more and more mechanized. The industries built up around building the war machines have generated a group of corporate conglomerates with capital that exceeds the GDP of many countries. Weapons industries have now surpassed energy, construction, and pharmaceutical companies to become the largest industries in the world. And no wonder, when a single Tomahawk cruise missile costs a million dollars.

A system has been set up between the various political bodies, weapons industries, and their lobbyists. Some call it the revolving door. It is what has become known as the military-industrial complex

Politicians can invest in the stocks of industries that they are responsible for allocating money to. They can act as consultants or advisors, or even sit on the board of a weapons manufacturer. It serves as a convenient way to get a politician on a corporation's payroll. Some politicians don't even wait to retire before they go to work for a Lockheed Martin, Boeing, or Northrup Grumman. These same industries are getting 90% or more of their money from government contracts (often no-bid), and are highly dependent on conflicts to create cash.

* * *

We must end endless wars that accomplish nothing but the waste of money and the murder of thousands. The first step is to be aware of how war propaganda and psychology work. Every war has public and private layers. The private layers (the profit motives) are always masked behind an acceptable public layer (the pretext under which the war is fought). Sadly, there are many who willingly accept whatever pretext they are fed. The propaganda doesn't have to be very sound, or even make sense. The official excuse for war is often presented as a moral high ground to justify the acts of imperialism.

Even then, A war supporter may not be terribly interested in questioning whether or not the propaganda is based on evidence or moral sincerity. Prejudice, a vicarious sense of masculinity, primitive base-level urges to dominate, conditioning, bigotry, party affiliation, or the hostility of an authoritarian personality are all factors that can to contribute to a person's devotion to war.

Here's one example: it seems obvious that the US had no interest in liberating the Kurds when they invaded Iraq. This was one of the many insincere rationales offered as grounds for the war. The reason there is such a large Kurdish population in Northern Iraq in the first place is because they fled there as refugees from Turkey. In 1997, at the peak of Turkey's ethnic cleansing, it was the second highest recipient of US aid in the world after Israel (which always comes in first).[14]

That Turkey and Israel both engage in ethnic cleansing is a non-issue. As long as the check comes back to the US arms industries, even if those funds ultimately came from US tax payers, none of the atrocities will ever be reported on TV. It doesn't matter if it's a Charles Taylor, Islam Karimov, Joseph Kony, Zine El Abidine Ben Al, Hosni Mubarak, or Than Shwe; the US media will turn a blind eye. The average American has never heard of any of these people, although they can recall names like Saddam Hussein, Bin Laden, Ahmadinejad, Gaddafi, and Bashar al-Assad.

Of all the reasons one might have for supporting war, party affiliation is the most baffling, because it ignores principles altogether. There were those who passionately supported Bush's wars and domestic spying programs, yet opposed Clinton or Obama for theirs. Likewise

[14] Israel's situation is not what it appears to be on the surface. Seventy-five percent of the aid sent to Israel is earmarked to be spent on US weapons. In 2000, Israel spent $1.8 billion of its $3 billion in aid on Lockheed Martin alone. Israel is a cash cow for the MIC, a medium through which the vested interests can increase their arm sales.

there were those who passionately opposed Bush's wars and spying, but would ignore or even rationalize why Obama continued those very same policies, or even expanded them. An action ought to be determined wrong or right based on what it is and the effects it has, not on who is carrying it out.

Poisoning children with depleted uranium is wrong because of the horrible birth defects it creates in newborns, and the slow, agonizing death it randomly brings to anyone within its range. The immorality of its use must be the same whether it's under the banner of an Obama or a Bush. The children will still die a horrible death regardless. To take the example further if purposely starving millions to death was wrong under Stalin during WWII, then why wasn't it also wrong when the British did the same thing in Bengal during the very same war? How about when the policies of the IMF create debt in order to profit corporations, even when it means pushing innocent people into abject poverty? This ability to blithely say "It's not wrong when WE do it," is both mind- blowing and tragic.

Vast numbers of people pick sides based not on the situation at hand but on the beliefs they attribute to the side they oppose. Peace advocates might not hate a particular war because of its gratuitousness, immorality, or monetary costs, but because they associate the pro-war side with greedy, old white guys and the ills of westernism.

On the flip side, do war advocates really believe that our nation's security is threatened? Do they believe that the military's mission is one of liberation, rather than securing resources or furthering someone's financial interests? Perhaps they just oppose the West-bashing that's now so fashionable with the kooks in the peace movement. Or perhaps it's simply a case of wanting to be on the winning team.

People support or oppose wars for all the wrong reasons, just as they support political candidates for all of the same wrong reasons. It's become a contest of image over substance. If psychology is allowed to override philosophy, then we consign our fate to the control of the public-relations piper. Throughout history, that has always been a dangerous place to be.

CHAPTER 19

The Wealth Gap

"Conservatism is not about tradition and morality, hasn't been for many decades... It is about the putative biological and spiritual superiority of the wealthy."

- Greg Bear

The richest 85 people in the world own as much as the bottom 3.5 billion.[120] Wealth disparity has grown to shocking[121] proportions, especially in the United States. It is hard to disagree with the idea that, if a person works harder and longer, they deserve to earn more than someone who does not. Unfortunately, it is no longer the case that those who show the most intelligence, talent, or industriousness are the ones making the most money.

The two key advantages when it comes to money- making at the very top are one's connections to government and a pre-existing condition of affluence. After all, it takes money to make money. Currently, only one percent of America holds 50% of the nation's wealth, while the bottom 80% retains a mere 7%. Not to worry; there is a path upwards. One of the best jobs you can get to ensure that you gain the status of millionaire is to become a member of Congress. 47% of today's congress members are millionaires – a level of wealth shared by only 1% of the rest of the country.[122]

Some of their fortunes are even larger, totaling in the hundreds of millions of dollars,[123] such as Michael McCaul (chairman of Homeland Security), John Kerry, Jane Harman, Mark Warner, Jay Rockefeller, Dianne Feinstein, Darrell Issa, Vern Buchanan, Jared Polis, and Herb Kohl. Some of the people on this list earn nearly half a billion dollars a year.

John Kerry, now Secretary of State under Obama, was formerly the chair of the Senate Foreign Relations Committee. While holding this post he made $294.9 million a year. He also sat on the Armed Services Committee, which gave him both political and financial advantages for insider trading.

 Jane Harman, now retired, agreed to lobby the Department of Justice (DOJ) to reduce charges against officials of the American Israel Public Affairs Committee (AIPAC) after they were caught spying against the United States. By the time she finished her time as a congresswoman, she was taking home $435.4 million a year.

Other congressmen also pull down figures in the tens of millions, including Nancy Pelosi, Gary Miller, Diane Lynn Black, Rodney Frelinghuysen, Rick Berg, Nita M. Lowey, Richard Blumenthal, Frank R. Lautenberg, Bob Corker, and Olympia J. Snowe.

Like all businesses, the state exists to make profit for itself and its subsidiaries. It is not concerned for the interests of the American people, but for the corporate interests of the fascist regime. Our congressmen only care about the public interest insofar as it overlaps with the objectives of their own careers. As John Cusack once put it in an interview, the government is acting like a giant ATM machine, and mainly for the war industries. They always lie to you. They spy on you. They will gladly send you or your child off to die for the state.[124]

Today, 40% of US workers make less than a full-time minimum-wage worker made in 1968. According to the Social Security Administration, a full 40.28% of all workers were making less than $20,000 a year in 2011.[125]

The solution is not as simple as raising the minimum wage. That would lead to price inflation, putting a strain on small businesses, while big businesses would have even more incentive to send jobs overseas, where the labor would be comparatively cheaper.

A better idea, counterproductive though it might sound, would be to cut taxes on businesses. The common straw-man argument against this is that cutting taxes is a trickle-down economics solution that doesn't work. The crucial element which gets ignored here, however is the word "business." Cutting capital gains on businesses – places with actual employees –benefits the business, which invariably benefits its workers.

There is no benefit for the economy to cut taxes on the rich, however. An individual's wealth does not have a direct correlation to their benefit to society; being wealthy does not automatically mean one is a job creator, for example. The majority of the richest people in the US or world are speculators, and don't actually produce anything. What we need are a lot more businesses, and a lot less gambling with the money of businesses. As we have seen, the financial institutions, the investment banks and the rating agencies will sooner lie and turn to the government to save them from the inevitable consequences of their theft and fraud. In a real business, the money that it realizes in profit becomes reinvested back into the economy.

Thomas Sowell pointed out in Capitalism Magazine: Those who imagine that profits first benefit business owners — and that benefits only belatedly trickle down to workers — have the sequence completely backward.

When an investment is made, whether it is to build a railroad or to open a new restaurant, the first money is spent hiring people to do the work. Without that, nothing happens.[126]

Parasites like Warren Buffet appear on TV whenever they want and preach about the necessity of a bailout for Goldman Sachs and other crooks, because they are deeply tied to their continued existence.[127] Buffet had tens of billions riding on the bailouts, so of course he advocated the doomsday scenario.[128]

 The words "conflict of interest" were never uttered. It is better for the restaurant owner, the hotel owner, shopkeeper, organic farmer, or who have you, to keep their money and invest it. Instead we live in a society where as much as 30% of it is stolen by the government, awarded to the likes of Lockheed Martin and used to build weapons designed to bomb innocent people on the other side of the ocean.

As I wrote in a previous book:

"We are suffering from a disease. Offshore slavery, sweat shops, exploited labor, insider trading, profiteering, debt slavery, predatory lending, avoidable starvation, and a blind eye to the rape, theft, murder and torture of the Third World are kept afloat by a steady combination of consumerism and sticking our heads in the sand. No one cares about people; not like they care about shiny things.

Our nation judges its well being by the stock market or its billionaire companies and not on the welfare of the general public, our physical and psychological well-being. Humanity is under the boot of the mighty dollar because of its association with self-worth.

Celeb-head, fashion conscious, herds scramble for the monthly slick magazines of plastic people 500 hundred self ranking quizzes, 400 g-spot articles, and cartoon-symbol horoscopes vaguely about themselves, like junkies so desperate for attention and direction that any superstition will do.

Daily fed pop-star trash, voyeuristic reality shows, and talk-show gossip fill the ears with utter nonsense distraction, and behind every shiny smiling buy-my-stuff billboard are unmentioned gravestones, and countless victims of imperialism. Give us this day our daily beautiful person with troubles. Ratings demand diva dramas not news about the world. We only feed the pigs slop, and why not? After all they keep eating it.

You get what you deserve by taking whatever is offered. Macho man vehicles, business bitch bravo, show everyone how much you paid. It's not the immoral, government assisted profit-at- all-cost corporations to blame, it's (you) the public, the consumers, for purchasing all their worthless hype and propaganda, the digital demands... " [15]

For all our complaining about government and big business, what the country desperately needs is a psychological shift, preferably one that focuses on fostering personal responsibility and accountability for our actions, regardless of our social or economic standing. As the late Libertarian Lakota Indian Russell Means might say, "Freedom requires responsibility."

---

[15] [15] Welcome to the USSA: corruption in the government and media, unearthing the Neocon camarilla

CHAPTER 20

Guns, Gays and God

"Panem et circenses."[16]

– Juvenal, Roman Satirist

---

[16] Lit. "Bread and circuses".

Sadly, the nation is not dividing over a debate between war and peace, the sixteen-trillion dollar debt, the slow erosion of our civil liberties, inflation, the cost of living, or the lack of jobs. Instead, the country's single most divisive issue is the debate around gay marriage. Okay, fine. Let's talk about it.

The government should have nothing to do with who a person is allowed to marry, heterosexual, homosexual or otherwise. If the government was not responsible for granting special privileges to married couples, there would not be an issue. Marriage is a social affair which should not need validation from the state.

And, yes, church has the right to enforce its own views on marriage – if you choose to follow its precepts, that is. In the end, you don't have to be a member of that church. If you disagree with their views on marriage, perhaps it's not really a great fit for you, anyway.

Religion, on the other hand, also does not have a monopoly on the institution of marriage, or love, for that matter. Why should anyone care what official sanctification is bestowed upon whatever kind of couple you happen to be? The same-sex marriage issue is really a watershed moment for the social approval of homosexuality.

It's is a way to get external validation for an act that has been traditionally taboo in our culture, at least for the past few centuries. These kinds of issues should be left to philosophical debate, not to opposing sides playing tug-of-war with legality and political approval. You cannot legislate morality. You cannot legislate the pathways of a person's thoughts. Social changes must be rooted in social thinking. That is the proper arena for any lasting cultural shifts.

Personally, I don't care who marries who, or if they marry at all; to each their own. But so long as there are special legal and economic privileges afforded to married couples, then marriage must be afforded to all. There is no law of man that should require a person's happiness be dependent on the approval of a church.

* * *

Freedom of religion is an inalienable right. People have the right to not eat pig, forego electricity, avoid alcohol, avoid shellfish, talk to their hands, spend thousands of dollars to put a dead body in a box, wear strange hats, dunk babies under water, eat symbolic wafers and drink magical grape juice, and utter mantras to help a sports team win. That is their right, regardless of how silly these things might seem to someone who doesn't subscribe to the same dogma.

It has become quite fashionable to bash religions. People will target a particular belief's most extreme tenets, and then use them as justification to throw the baby out with the bath water. This isn't to say that religious ideologies should be held above criticism, of course. They deserve the same share of critical analysis that any other philosophy must endure.

But there is a huge difference between attacking the ideas of a faith, and attacking the people of a faith. For example, I can dislike the habit of smoking without hating the smoker who lights up. I can dislike a particular song without hating those who listen to it. A person is a lot more than just a single bad habit or his bad taste in music.

Islam should not be judged by the havoc wrought by the Boston bombers, any more than any religion, race or subsection of the population be singled out for the crimes perpetrated by a single member of that group. Otherwise, in shootings alone, Christianity could be vilified for the murders committed by Anders Brievik in Norway; Judaism, for those in Tuscon and Columbine; Asians for Virginia Tech; and autistic people for Sandy Hook. Whatever punishment should be meted out in an individual case does not carry over to the whole.

Thus the fact that some religious people may indeed hold prejudice toward homosexuals does not mean that prejudice is the sole product of their faith. Some atheists may hold the same view for their own reasons without the need for supernatural rhetoric. That there are passages in the Bible that condemn homosexuality does not mean that that is how all Christians practice their faith.

The Bible also preaches the divine right of kings, the need   for animal   sacrifice,   and   forbids   wearing clothing made of two kinds of cloth. Nobody is seriously calling for a return to a monarchy, painting our doors with the blood of sheep, or making sure nobody wears a cotton/acrylic blend t-shirt. Religion doesn't make a person good or bad, it's the other way around; the actions of the individual tarnish the name of their religion. Many still blame their faith when they want to justify what they already believe, anyway (a common failing shared by pollsters, statisticians, and politicians).

This is why one will find people of the same faith range from those who their lives to serving the poor to others who will cheerfully spend church money on digging up diamonds in Africa, as the televangelist, Pat Robertson, did.[129]

There is also unapologetic prejudice toward the non- religious in the US. As Jesse Ventura pointed out in a Playboy interview,[130] an openly atheist person cannot get elected in the United States. You can advocate war, express misogynist or racist views, or even admit to an affair, but profess your singular lack of faith in the supernatural and you will lose any chance of winning an election. As with racism, homosexuality and other forms of prejudice, the stigma attached atheism will fade with time. There are areas within the US, however, which are just as bigoted towards people who do have faith. Just ask a Catholic in northern California.

* * *

Even more than religion, the relative merits of a firearm depend on the user. They can protect people or be used offensively. A semi-automatic version can defend an individual against superior numbers, but just as easily be used to go on a killing spree at a school. The crimes committed with guns have led to an ongoing, heated debate over whether the private

citizen should retain the right to possess firearms. Here's the thing: as with illegal drugs, criminals can get guns if they really want to. Outlawing firearms wouldn't have stopped any of those school shootings, and the gunmen would have gotten their hands on the guns they wanted regardless of the law.

The two countries with the lowest rates of violent crime and shootings are Japan and Switzerland. While Japan has (almost) no guns at all and Switzerland has more than anyone else, people of both countries manage to not kill each other. Mexico, like Japan, also bans guns while the US allows them, and these two countries have incredibly high crime rates. Countries stretching from Columbia to the USA have incredibly high death rates from firearms regardless of their laws, all of which outlaw guns other than the US, because of the war on drugs. It is that and not the access or lack of access to guns that is causing the problem.

The claims that guns, or the lack thereof, lead to crime are erroneous. Poverty leads to crime; It has nothing to do with the available tool. The perception that they have no future is the reason smart, young loners on psychotropic drugs shoot up schools. If it wasn't a gun, they could just as easily use a good, old-fashioned melée weapon, a homemade bomb, or even a car or bus. The varieties of weapons are myriad; you can't ban everything.

Without a doubt the intelligence agency assisted "drug war" has created a climate of violence among the poor who are tempted to engage in this illegal and dangerous business of dealing drugs because of its high potential rewards. It is a potential way out of poverty.

Instead of blaming the AR-15 used in the Sandy Hook shooting, let's have a look at the person who pulled the trigger and the society that produced him. If it hadn't been an AR-15, it might have been be two pistols, as it was in the Virginia Tech shooting (where the shooter racked up 32 kills – six more than Sandy Hook). The TV media would like you to think the latest one is the most heinous. They assume you lack the sense to look it up, or the memory to recall previous incidents. In any case, I don't think it's the privilege of the press to rank their deadliness.

Without a gun, the only people we render defenseless are the law-abiding citizens. I do not want to create a situation where my grandmother cannot defend herself or her property if someone breaks into her house to rob her. Disarming the public will create targets.

America has had guns for hundreds of years. It didn't have school shootings until the introduction of prescription SSRI drugs to children. It's the neglected acting out not the abused and they are always on these drugs. A few Hellos might have done more good than masking a sick person's symptoms with zombie pills.

School shootings or mass shootings resonate with more people because the victims are random. They or their kids could be victims. Other shootings in the US tend to be gang or drug related so as long as they are not involved in those things they don't really need to worry about them. Having a gun at home makes them feel safe from break ends. But people using guns at school makes people not feel safe. This is the reason that those type of shootings motivate more people to get active than the common every day shootings that happen in big cities.

I don't own any guns and in general I am just not a fan of them. But from looking at other places with a similar culture and drug war which have banned guns I see no evidence that this makes any difference to criminals. Brazil has over 60k gun murders a year it has a population that is about the same size as the US. Other countries have other cultures and you can see that play out in other laws.

For example, heroin is just as illegal in Japan as it is Britain but Britain as a huge opium problem and Japan does not. The drug culture simply isn't ripe in Japan. Why that is has a complex answer. On the flipside, even though it is illegal to not pay people for overtime work, this happens in Japan all the time. Workers must "volunteer" to work after hours for free, if not they will be replaced by someone who will. This is also illegal in the US but people are not working themselves to death, which literally happens in Japan. Generally, although not perfectly, overtime work is given overtime pay or at least regular pay in the US. The point is, just making something illegal doesn't make the problem go away when there is a deep cultural issue at work. So making crass comparisons on a single data point is asinine.

Also the US had the same guns in the 1980s yet only one school shooting and that was in 1989. All but one of these mass shootings has been done by a person who didn't have a father in the home. This stat also has a majority correlation with regular gun murders. So maybe if we didn't subsidize broken homes, there would be fewer of them. We do not have enough information about that, since from 1980 to Feb 2018 there have only been 96 mass shootings, that is 3 or more people killed. The sample is too small. I do think that the solution needs to be many changes about many things. Do we really need to dope kids up on psychotropic drugs are early as 3rd grade? Shouldn't we have some red flags by now since these shooters have such similar profiles? Is the media sensationalism in their coverage looked at as a means in the eyes of a shooter to add significance to their death, as all but three of these attackers killed themselves? What changed culturally so much between the 80s to now? Maybe it is all of these above, media hype, loner, no father, on SSRI drugs, and has access to a gun, and one sees the red flag. But yes gun control in my opinion should focus more on the daily shootings than on these rare events. The left is so adamant about blaming the tool, and the right is so bent on defending the tool, that solutions for all these shootings outside of the parameters of gun regulation never see the light of day.

CHAPTER 21

America's Mechanized Terrorists

"With the NDAA, his failure to close Guantanamo Bay and the ramping use of drones, President Obama looks suspiciously like President Bush, a man on a quest for American Empire."

– Justin Sane, lead singer of Anti-flag

As if there weren't enough reasons against disarming the public already, the government's growing investment in drone warfare should be reason enough. Drones are unmanned, remote- controlled, aerial weapons that can spy on and kill people from great distances. They've not only been used to kill foreign enemies of the US regime, they've even been used to kill Americans.

President Obama authorized the murder of a religious cleric, Anwar al-Awlaki,[131] and his 16-year old, American-born son, Abdulrahman al-Awlaki,[132] when he added their names to his executive kill list. Both men were killed in two separate drone strikes. The latter strike also resulted in the deaths of a number of other Yemeni teenagers, including Abdulrahman's 17-year-old cousin. And in a day and age where the president is allowed to call for the deaths of anyone he deems a threat, drones have now been approved to patrol inside the US as well.

Things could get much worse, though. In Pakistan, for example, the frustrated reaction to the drone strikes was to kill several non-

Muslims in a suicide bombing, and the US responded with yet another drone strike. Drones are able to fire a kill shot from miles away; since their targets can't fire back, the most extreme among the victims take it out on innocent people in a desperate hope it will stop future strikes. All this does is create a gradually escalating, vicious cycle of never-ending retaliation.

It doesn't take a political analyst to see the accumulation of hatred this will create in the future, inciting the suicide bombers to move their efforts from Pakistan to the US as the drone strikes persist. And make no mistake: the drone strikes are not killing terrorists. The US has announced on multiple occasions a successful kill, only to have that person show up later still very much alive. One particular Al Qaeda member has the unique distinction of having been killed eight times. The only people the US actually manages to kill on a regular basis are guiltless families, wedding parties, funeral attendees,[133] and even the occasional school,[134] none of whom had a single tie to terrorism.

There will soon be ground drones as well. These will be able to enter into proxy wars on behalf of the United States, where until now it has relied on rent-a- terrorists to avoid risking American soldiers (as it did in Syria). And make no mistake: there will be blowback. Drone technology will spread to every nation, the same way airplanes, submarines and nuclear bombs did. Technology cannot be contained.

The more mechanized war becomes, the more quickly wars of choice will begin. The problem is, what goes around comes around. All empires eventually fall. The last century alone saw the fall of five great empires: the Austrian-Hungarian empire, the Ottoman the British, the

French and the USSR.

The US rose to become a military super power after the Europeans destroyed each other during the world wars. It has had its time and is now repeating the same militaristic and financial mistakes that past empires made before their own collapses. Is there time to turn things around? Yes, but it will not be easy. In December of 2013, after an American drone murdered 17 people in a wedding procession,[135] the parliament of Yemen finally banned drones from their air space. Time will tell as to whether the US pays attention to the law.

I believe we can defeat the leeches of empire whothrive on theft and the exploitation of foreign countries, and restore the Republic without a collapse

The advantage we have now that has never existed before is the internet. People today, at least for the time-being, can freely share ideas and information, even with the likes of the NSA listening in. It has been the video-sharing sites, the blogs, the message boards and the social networks that have led to revolutions in the Middle East, South America, Iceland, parts of mainland Europe and perhaps, very soon, in Egypt.

With tools like these, we are beginning to build a viable alternative to the corporate media. It is thanks to these tools that the US's reporting on drone strikes has failed so miserably. Everyday people are free to go online to expose and debunk the mainstream media with their own sources of information, or publish first-hand accounts that would never be carried on the TV news.

Illustration by Cailean Babcock

Concept by Ryan Dawson

This kind of attitude is psychologically crippling. They keep their narrative intentionally vague, too, never giving you many names or documentation. Instead they toss around important-sounding terms like "New World Order",[136] "globalists", and sometimes even more ridiculous things like "Luciferians" or "Illuminati". These kinds of generic paths to nowhere serve as little more than conspiratainment. Fear sells,[137] but that is not the emotion patriots should be using to galvanize a movement. What we need is will.

The government is, by and large, a bunch of frail, weak old men, the majority of which are not very well-educated or possess any special skills. Most congressmen do not read the bills they support because they would not understand them.[138] They rely heavily on twenty-something-year old legislative assistants just to manage their own offices. They have no idea how to manage a nation and have become nothing more than dysfunctional yes-men to the lobbies.

We can beat these people. The only advantage they have is the mass media, which controls the elections. It propagates authoritarianism and fear to keep the system together. If we place all our eggs in one basket, let it be in building a true, independent media, free of sensationalism and fear mongering.

Going forward, our goals should be to end the Federal Reserve System, withdraw from all wars and occupations (direct or by proxy), cut our enormous government waste, and uphold the Constitution. We have no need for three-letter institutions like the DHS TSA, NSA, BIS or MIC. Step one in winning the psych war is the creation of a new media. It will not take as much money as it may seem. We don't even need a fraction of the cost compared to those we are up against because it's far more expensive to produce a lie than to tell the truth. The truth is on our side and it will prevail if it has a chance to be heard.

This is why protecting the internet from censorship is absolutely vital in our struggle for justice. Support good web-based journalism. In these early days, the men and women producing podcasts and publishing blogs are supported through donations or work for free. We are only in the infancy of the online press, but if we support it, it could become the mainstream media of the future.

Telling the truth and defending justice might not always get you the most friends, but it will get you the right ones. Social and intellectual revolutions must predicate political revolution for anything worthwhile to last. We need to work towards an end to government borrowing, end corporate welfare, and keep the government out of the marketplace. What a wonderful world we could have. As Gandhi said, "Be the change you want to see in the world." We have the numbers and the ideas. You cannot stop an idea whose time has come.

CHAPTER 22

The Rise of Trump and the Identitarian Crybullies

"Reality is sexist" let's live in pretend land where feelings trump biology and if you don't agree then you're a Nazi"

Outgroup-directed moral outrage can be elicited in response to perceived threats to the ingroup's moral status. A study by two university psychology professors confers this hypothesis.[139]

This is a problem with collectivists. An SJW identifies themselves as a category rather than as an individual. As such they also blame acts done by individuals, states, or institutions, not on the ones responsible or their ideologies but on the categorical biological make up of the participants. A sense of guilt when it is their own category is one source for virtue singling.

The alt-right has a similar origin of their own identitarian psychology. They too see themselves as a biological category. Thus if Isaac Newton was white and they are white then their team is smarter than the others. How about, Newton is smarter than most of us because "we" didn't do jack squat. Exceptional individuals also arise out of particular economic systems. Would we have noticed the talents of an expert pianist if the piano did not exist first? How many writers would have never been if not for the simple invention of eye glasses?

You cannot attribute the achievements or tragedies done by individuals or institutions (like such and such company makes the best phone) to a biological teleology.

Oppression is the product of power not racial destiny. Many groups have colonized or dominated others. Many groups enslaved people, went to war and so on. The most determining factor of a civilization's success isn't its genes, it's free markets. Communism fails under every flag. Theocracy stagnates under every religion. Markets work because individualism works. Make something new first and get rich. It is that simple. Rewarding success works. Liberals do the opposite. They want to punish success and reward failure. They are constantly rewarding self defeating behavior. The idea is to assist people in need, but the result is reinforcing the bad attitudes and habits that cause need in the first place. Sure some people are just unlucky, there are natural disasters, and there are circumstances in life beyond a person's control. Many others however fail because of their own behavior.

The Liberals suffer from a stalking fear that allowing merit based outcomes will mean that there is inequality by category. Well, change your categories. Anyone can have merit, so the only categories are people with merit and people with entitlement. The breakdown of the degree of success between arbitrary biological, sexual, or sexual orientations, age, or geographic categories is irrelevant.

Profiteers and Cultural Marxist like to wear a do-gooder mask such as, the environment, health, or education, as they push their anti-western agenda. After all who is anti-health or anti-education? Those profiteering and the Social Justice Warriors championing their causes are not the same group. There are many useful rubes who can be whipped up into a frenzy to support policies that ultimately lead to labor exploitation, unemployment, downtrodden cities, and erosion of the first amendment. For example, people may support price controls or rent control to make things cheaper or guaranteed loans for higher education, without realizing that such loans make it more expensive and price controls drive away development and production which causes shortages, the very opposite of the desired results.

The same thing happens with immigration. It masks itself as a fight against xenophobia or racism. Well no one wants those labels aside from the few folks who actually are xenophobic and racist. Affirmative action, welfare, and fair gender pay, are promoted as fighting racism, classism, and sexism. Facts don't matter. The crybully tactic, to avoid criticism or even discussion, is to accuse the opposition loudly and collectively of horrible prejudices. If they can find some loon who actually is the Nazi-monster they portray to throw a camera on, then all the better. Discussion is shut down for ordinary people because no one wants the stigma associated with the isms crybullies obsessively chant. Likewise perhaps people guilty over their own, or previous prejudiced beliefs that they had to work through, will be attracted to witch hunting as it relieves them of a sense of guilt and publicly signals that they are no longer that way.

People not deep in politics, rally with great indignation in support of the masks without looking behind them. They don't want to because championing the political correctness is too psychologically gratifying. Failures are attracted to groups built around resentment. It's why inferiority complexes hate things seen as strong. An Authoritarian can exercise power and pass it off as selflessly protecting some other marginalized group usually from being offended.   After all isms are very bad things. And we are all for better education, health, environment, and things like equality and fairness. The problem is one cannot vaguely just be for a result such as good X. One has to know the methods and policies to achieve good X. This part is skipped, the leftist ideology wraps itself up in the aims and desired result and cries prejudice to anyone who doesn't agree with their methods. In fact, some go as far as to cast all outsiders as "Nazis" which is ridiculous.

There is nothing wrong or intrinsically xenophobic about opposing **illegal** immigration especially when there is a perfectly legal way to immigrate.

Affirmative action is itself racist, and in being so, actually sustains a racist reaction towards it as it forces people to have merit within their category and not across the board. That is discrimination. Plus it undermines and second guesses minorities who would have succeeded without it. If you lower the standards for certain biological categories then the result is their credentials will also be seen as having a lower standard. Employers are not blind, they will know the favoritism granted to favored classes. Creating a favored class out of fear of a favored class is not a well thought out solution. For more see Dr. Thomas Sowell talk about how affirmative action hurts minorities[140]

Not holding people to the same standards for schooling is what black authors like Larry Elder call "White condescension" of course they will adamantly profess that it's all just fighting racism while ignoring that the practice is itself racist. Liberals are so arrogant, paternalistic, and backhandedly condescending to minorities.

Affirmative action simultaneously appeals to white condescension and virtue signaling. It's opponents can be chastised as ignorant and racist. Its proponents can feel the psychological gratification of a sense of moral superiority and knowledge of cultural diversity, a very posh thing indeed. Measurable statistical data, over a period of decades, showing the harm that affirmative action has done has no place when it comes to climbing the smugness ladder.

The ultimate irony is the proponent with fingers in his ears is guilty of his own accusations, ignorance and racism. He is ignorant of how harmful Affirmative Action has been for those it professes to help, and

ignoring the intrinsic racism of a policy that replaced merit with merit
only within a limited racial category for some and merit only after
those categories have been filled, for everyone else.

 To relegate any disagreement to a policy as part of some social taboo
or stigma is just a form of bullying. In essence, saying agree with me
or you are a racist is a totally dishonest platform from its onset. If you
 cannot listen to reason and ideas first without making a pre-judgement,
 that is what we call prejudice.

Another example was the successful push to uphold Ebonics as
alternative grammar. If people cannot properly speak their first and
usually only language, then that is not conducive to success. But
rather than holding communities to the same standards as others are
held to and teaching, demanding and expecting that people use proper
English, or at least be able to, we get an embrace of ignorance and a
push to enable it,. All of this is done, while of course, as always,
labeling opposition to such a stupid thing as Ra-ra-ra-racist.

Welfare doesn't work. The programs have been around 40 years and it
does as Austrian economist predicted. Most of the money feeds an
administration. Failure is subsidized and that goes for both the poor
and the rich. Corporate welfare is theft on a larger scale. From top to
bottom, it creates moral hazard. Thomas Sowell breaks down
Welfare's results[141]

There is no gender pay gap. Men earn more on average, because they
work in professional fields more on average and they work more in the
same job longer on average. People who work more are supposed to
earn more. Doctors earn more than nurses. Doctors earn more than
other doctors too depending on the demand and specialization needed
in their field. To say that men earn more on average therefore women

have lower wages and salaries for the same work, is showing little other than how innumerate people are about statistics.

The NBA makes more than the WNBA because there is a greater demand for their product from the public. As a result NBA players earn far more than WNBA players because they are producing far more than WNBA players. It's not sexist to not have equal outcomes when there isn't equal effort or ability.[142] Adding up extremely above average salaries of professional athletes, in a field largely dominated by males, will offset averages between men and women. A few sports like Tennis where the demand for the product is closer the salaries are closer. Other male dominated professions like the military are not seeing females rise to the top to become generals so often if ever because simply not enough women bother entering such a profession and then it is a simple numbers game.

The extreme left is not interested in hearing disagreement, they want a safe space. The hypocrisy is thick because they provide anything but a safe space for opposition. They censor, protest and sloganeer over top of people on top of labeling them Nazis. All of it is ramping up towards normalizing violence. It's OK to break windows, assault people, and set things on fire so long as the temper tantrum is couched behind fighting an ism, including fascism. The funny thing is, the Antifa movement is itself fascist by both its physical assaults on property and people as well as its assaults on history, culture, and science. Yes, even science gets cry bullied now. In biology a gender is determined by genes not by feelings or tastes.

Sitting in the shadows are the profiteers. Some big businesses benefit from illegal immigration. The exploited labor is cheap and expendable. Simply by painting Kurdish forces, the same involved in head chopping, genital mutilation, and terrorism in Syria, as Socialists, has gathered them support from the unthinking left who along with Bernie Sanders and Hilary Clinton held tightly on to the "Assad Must Go" policy even when there has never been a plan proposed on what happens after that. Who would replace Assad and what disastrous results would that beget? Because you see, consequences don't matter to this ilk. Supporting a brand is what matters to them.

Three of the four people arrested for tearing down a statue of a Civil War soldier in Durham were all part of the communist party. They dont really care about the Civil War suddenly after 155 years. SJWs accept the cartoonish star wars version of the Civil War of good verse evil, denying the fact that the entire South was offered constitutional protection for slavery before secession through the Corwin amendment and yet they seceded anyway. That the war physically starts by South Carolina firing on the fort that was collecting the new import and export taxes, Fort Sumter, and the fact that the same state created a secession movement over the tariff issue in 1828 (when slavery was never even mentioned) doesn't matter to them. The real motivation for SJWs isn't about slavery. President Grant the main Union General had slaves. He's on the $50 bill and he also has statues. The real motivation is that SJWs hate conservatives and they hate the South because they hate red sates. The statues stood through two Obama presidencies, without issue. The entire outrage is a horde of leftist who are still butthurt about Trump being elected president.

*****

Civil War virtue signaling

The old axiom History is written by the winners, will soon need to be changed to History is written by the whiners. Closet communist and directionless youth incapable of accepting accountability or responsibility for personal failures are on a blame rage. What I see happening here is a group masking its deep seeded hate for western culture and the south in particular behind a wall of moral indignation. Dogmatic activists are using the weapon of yelling Nazi or hurling accusations of one ism or another to assault History and Science. Biology is now a matter of feelings and the cry-bully tactics have forced parents to allow boys in the girl's room in their children's schools.

A generation raised on Hollywood, have now turned the complexities of the American Civil War into a childish narrative of good vs. evil fought to liberate slaves. Thus from that ignorant perspective any and all symbols of Southern culture despite over a century and a half of acceptance, must be and could only be symbols of racism and so they need to be destroyed or removed. Antifa have vandalized private property, prevented free speech, assaulted people, and advocate communism. The red in their flag stands for communism. They have red and black because they paradoxically are anarchist and communist. Essentially they just don't want any form of hierarchy because hierarchy means admitting there is a superior and inferior, and not everyone gets a trophy. CNN, the identitarian pulpit, added fuel to the fire. Closet communist breaking windows and setting fire to things hitting cars with bats and throwing trash cans, macing people, and flinging piss and dog shit in an adolescent temper tantrum is ignored by the fake news. Possibly people who normally would not otherwise, are supporting Trump out of sheer spite against the crybullies, since he is seen as the lesser evil.

No one wants to deal with the stigma of being accused of being a racist other than actual racists. Thus a very very small group of useful idiots preach white nationalism while wearing Klan hoods and waving Nazi flags. They showed up at a "unite the right" rally in Charlottesville in August of 2017. Peaceful protest against removing a statue of Robert E Lee had been going on for months by Virginians without any coverage, but that wasn't brought up. Of course the cameras focused on the racist fools, practically all of whom did not live in Charlottesville, because it fit the race-baiting narrative they literally wanted to sell. These "racial realist" also like to wave the banners of the confederate battle flag, the US flag, and the holy cross of Christianity. These people do not monopolize what these symbols mean or have meant for more than a century before they were born. But for an SJW or an Ethnic nationalist, everything is always about race. The Alt-Reich white nationalist losers who live action shit posted in Charlottesville, took a real issue about preserving a park and a statue of Robert E Lee, a Virginian who prevented cities like Charlottesville from being burned to the ground by an invading army, and made it about themselves.

Ironically they hold and preach the same views as President Lincoln who Lee was fighting. Lincoln held that the white race, and in his mind the superior race, should not mix with inferior races. That white nationalists would parade around confederate flags, crosses, and American flags, does not make them the sole representatives of those symbols. The KKK is not the South just as ISIS is not the Muslims. A black street gang is not the blacks. A Zionist is not the Jews. A gunman is not all gun owners. An illegal is not the Mexicans. Attributing tragedies or accomplishments to biological categories needs to end.

What has allowed the live action shit posters (LASP) to LARP (live action role play) about and hijack the flag? The media has. Stories of race/sex are click bait. Even the dumbest and weakest person can pat themselves on the back for the simple act of not being racist, hardly a feat in the current year. Every time there is a meth-head neo-Nazi waving a confederate flag he gets a camera. It also shows they are as ignorant about History as they are about race. They do not speak for the South as a culture or Virginia in particular. When president Trump pointed out this very simple nuance, the press, the same press that supported actual neo-Nazis in Ukraine, acted like president Trump supported racists. All he did was pop the bubble of propaganda the press was deceptively painting of a clash between racists and antiracists. I support the preservation of Lee Park and all historical statues and the greater issue facing the whole country.

President Trump has become a symbolic president in this culture war. Immediately, as Trump was being sworn in, Antifa was in DC destroying property and all throughout the election they screamed racist, sexist, xenophobic, bigot, any ism label you can think of at Donald Trump. They basically got him elected because the general disgust towards the fascist professional-shamers hiding behind political correctness were seen by the majority as the greater evil.

It is also ironic that people can condemn racism and then in the same breath say completely absurd and racist things about white people. White people enslaved the Africans (and other whites) white people killed the Indians (and other whites) white people were the Nazis (who were stopped largely by other whites) is what you will hear in a list of grievances usually from white people themselves who feel a need to check their privilege. They fail to see that institutions like slavery were globally practiced by every race. It was Western civilization the same they like to blame for slavery and start and stop the story of slavery within those parameters, who actually ended slavery in their own nations and then went about forcing an end to it globally. Slavery was an act of governments not races. Race based slavery is rather new by comparison as traveling to other continents was not easy or cost efficient in the past. Normally places enslaved whoever was next door.

The English word slave is derived from the word Slav because so many Slavs were captured and enslaved. Basic geography gave Western Europe advantages over the East. One has coastal sea ports and the other doesn't. In the Middle East barring a brief period under Cyrus the Great, in China, Africa India, and Native Mexico it was all the same way where conquered people were turned into slaves.

 In modern times it was western civilization and culture where universal suffrage first arose. New Zealand was the first place women could vote and this spread first through western European civilization and then to others. Equal rights still hasn't taken root in many places outside of western civ. But the Social Justice Warrior, rather than recognizing these achievements of western philosophy and culture, instead exclusively blames them for having ever practiced something bad while ignoring the same practice done across the globe.

Any Historian worth his salt will tell you that despite all the horrible wars between Native Americans and Europeans in America, what killed the Indian was Small Pox. Now there were instances of bio warfare. People were well aware of it. Even George Washington wrote about this, as they suspected that the British of using that tactic in the Revolutionary War. People didn't need a specific knowledge of germs and microorganisms to understand contamination by contact. However, the drive against American Indians was not the result of a racial **teleology** of evil white genes. It was the result of an evil **ideology**, in this case religion with extreme prejudice, that served as a mask to justify wealth and land acquisition.

What allows one group to succeed where another fails is not racial superiority it is market superiority. Nothing could exemplify this more than the two Koreas which until the 1950s were not separated. That means they have the same race and same language and much of the population is older than the separation and yet the outcomes could not be more different. Race obsessed folks on the Alt-Right have a fetish for IQ statistics. Well in the Koreas the IQ and genes are basically the same. But one side cannot feed itself and relies on the world food program for calorie bars. This of course doesn't work as you have a hermit nation suffering from too much government, relying on an international government program for food, so naturally people have starved to death in mass. On the other side, South Korea, has the 11th largest economy in the world. Some of you might be reading this as an e-book on a Smartphone made in South Korea. None of you are reading this from anything made in North Korea. However let's hope things change. For the edgy commie who doesn't live in a communist nation and never has, writing rants in their rooms on their private property, North Korea is a wonderful place and the bad things said about it are either all propaganda, or it's only in bad shape because of everyone else. Sanctions hurt them, they say. Yes, I agree, they need to have trade. They need to be able to buy and sell things with others…what's that called again? Oh yeah, capitalism.

Chapter 23

"It is better to debate a question without settling it than to settle a question without debating it." - Joseph Joubert

Open for Debate

Televised presidential debates have been the most important and pivotal part of the presidential election process since JFK defeated Nixon. Carter's victory over Ford, followed by Reagan's victory over Carter, were largely thanks to how public opinion was swayed by the outcome of each candidate's presidential debates.

Perhaps more important was when Ross Perot, a third party candidate, got into the debates and ended up walking away with some 20% of the votes, mainly from potential voters for George Bush, Sr., thus allowing Bill Clinton to win. A third party candidate had never done so well. Perot's success was not just because of the power of his personal wealth to fund his campaign, but also because he brought up important issues that neither corporate-backed party would have addressed otherwise.

Third parties have always been important in the American political climate, even when they don't win They put issues on the table that the Democrats and Republicans have subsequently been forced to co-opt in order to retain votes. Universal suffrage, the abolition of slavery, public education, the direct election of senators, the formation of labor unions, unemployment compensation and many other major issues were all introduced into the political arena by third parties.

Sadly, there hasn't been a third party candidate allowed in the debates since Perot's appearance in 1992. Pat Buchannan in 2000, and Ralph Nader in 2000 and 2004, were both refused access to the debates. (Ralph Nader was refused despite having qualified to be on the ballots in 43 states and Washington, DC.)

Later, even candidates from the major parties, such as Dennis Kucinich (D) Mike Gravel (D) and Ron Paul (R), were in effect, all but invisible in the debates during the primaries, due to their anti-war stance. All of the debate time and attention went to pro-war hawks such as Hilary Clinton, Barack Obama and John McCain.

To find the root cause for this policy of excluding valid candidates from the debates, one has only to follow the money. In the past, the networks financed the debates; later, control passed to the nonpartisan League of Women Voters. However, since 1988, all of the debates have been controlled by the "Republicrats".

In the 1980s, the Democrats and Republican secretly drafted what is called the "Memorandum of Understanding," in which they agreed to work together to exclude other candidates, as well as to veto and control which journalists were allowed to ask them questions, and on what subjects.

In October of 1988, Nancy Neuman, speaking on behalf of the League of Women Voters, stated, "The League of Women Voters is announcing today that we have no intention of becoming an accessory to the hoodwinking of the American public. Under these circumstances the league is withdrawing its sponsorship of the presidential debates."[143] Since that time, the Commission on Presidential Debates, or CPD, has been in charge. It was created by the chairmen of the two major parties, Frank Fahrenkopf Jr. and Paul Kirk, Jr.

Under secretive contracts, the two parties and the commission they created conspire to eliminate the threat of competition from other parties, and to avoid engaging in actual debate. They have scripted answers to pre-screened questions presented by a moderator selected by the two parties. The debates have devolved to nothing more than a tightly controlled performance. Candidates no longer challenge each other, and there are no spontaneous questions.

George Farah, author of No Debate: How the Republican and Democratic parties Secretly Control the Debates, called it a corporate carnival. I concur with his assessment.[144] A growing number of Americans also seem to be aware of what a farce the debates have become. As the numbers of those watching the debates has dropped by half, voter turnout has also continued to decline. The Carter-Reagan debate had

60% viewership; by the time of Bush, Jr. vs. Gore, it had dropped to less than 30%. The CPD's sponsorship list reads like a who's-who of corporations. Unsurprisingly, the modern candidate refuses to venture outside of his corporate-approved circles.

Perhaps what is needed is the creation of a citizens' debate commission, as outlined by such activist NGOs as Open Debates or the Citizens Debate Commission. Another solution may be to allow things to continue in the direction they seem to already be going, which is to nullify the importance of the presidential debates on TV.

As transparent and staged as they have become, perhaps it would be better to move the public's focus to the more even-handed arena of the internet. Campaign finances are already being raised through the internet, and video sharing sites are enjoying an exponentially increased role in presenting the candidate platforms as the value of the internet as a community forum continues to increase.

As the 'news' becomes more and more partisan, and as the three letter networks continue to promote fake news like "Russian hackers" and gotcha stories Ebola could outbreak at any moment, they will become obsolete. They are on their way out. The new battle is with internet sensationalism.

Chapter 24
Torture

"It's the publicity function of Amnesty that I think has made its name so widely known, not only to readers in the world, but to governments – and that's what matters.." -Peter Benenson

Is there any purpose for torture? The ticking time bomb scenario is the best justification the pro torture camp can come up with and this line of thought has been propped up by propaganda in Hollywood with shows like 24. In reality this isn't anything but a hypothetical situation. Time and time again torture has been shown to produce nothing but unreliable information. People will lie or confess to anything to make the pain stop. This is how we have so many recorded confessions of witchcraft. Obviously no one was actually a witch or had magic powers, but they will say anything under torture.

This talk of torturing information out of people is still limiting the issue. The real world use of torture by the United States hasn't even been for gaining information. They have done it for entertainment and sadistic fun. Detainee in Iraq were severely tortured. Everyone wants to forget about Abu Ghraib. Children were raped in front of their mothers and their screams were recorded for a rape sound track. This was played for their mothers to hear at night. The mothers were passing notes asking for the men to come kill them. Seymour Hersh gave a speech to the ACLU explaining:

"Some of the worst things that happened you don't know about, okay? Videos, um, there are women there. Some of you may have read that they were passing letters out, communications out to their men. This is

at Abu Ghraib ... The women were passing messages out saying 'Please come and kill me, because of what's happened' and basically what happened is that those women who were arrested with young boys, children in cases that have been recorded. The boys were sodomized with the cameras rolling. And the worst above all of that is the soundtrack of the boys shrieking that your government has. They are in total terror. It's going to come out."

"...I can also tell you written complaints were made to the highest officers and so we're dealing with a enormous massive amount of criminal wrongdoing that was covered up at the highest command out there and higher, and we have to get to it and we will. We will."[145]

Former detainee Kasim Hilas said in their testimony that:[146]

"I saw [name blacked out] fucking a kid, his age would be about 15-18 years. The kid was hurting very bad and they covered all the doors with sheets. Then when I heard the screaming I climbed the door because on top it wasn't covered and I saw [blacked out], who was wearing the military uniform putting his dick in the little kid's ass, I couldn't see the face of the kid because his face wasn't in front of the door. And the female soldier was taking pictures."

The audio of the child rape soundtrack was played for select members of Congress... They largely kept this under wraps as Fox News did damage control of pictures that were being leaked out of naked prisoners stacked on top of each other. Therey were treated no worse than cheerleaders. the lawyer for the torturers proclaimed in court.[147]

The press ignored this and made a heated debate about water boarding, thus limiting the real scope of torture while covering up all but the most mild end of it. By arguing endlessly about whether or not water boarding (originally called Chinese water torture) was considered torture or not they were effectively pretending like this was the torture that was going on and none of the other things like sodomizing children in front of their mothers had happened.

The majority f the evidence of women and girls being gang raped and boys being sodomized, people beaten and dragged around on the floor with leases like dogs is of course "classified." It is not classified because of any real national security secrets or ways and means for gather intelligence. It is classified because it is illegal and embarrassing. This is the government. And it is not only the US government that enables, and covers up torture.

To get around what little resistance there is to torture, the CIA simply used the rendition program. A rendition is when the CIA simply takes detainees to a country where torture is legal and tortures them over there.

Honestly if there is anything close to being worse than mass murder it is mass torture and rape, and in the case of the pointless US invasion of Iraq we got all of the above, torture rape and murder. The Israeli synarchy behind the push for that war is becoming more well known as time goes by. American support for religious fanatics be they Zionist in Israel or Wahhabi in Saudi Arabia will be a dark stain in History. Ultimately there is no one to blame for the torture and cover up other than the government itself. A few people were prosecuted but only because they were brazen enough to take pictures and some of these got out to the public. This Hell on Earth isn't isolated to Abu Ghrabi either. America's ongoing war in Afghanistan, which is now the US's longest war which a multitude of other nations participate in, is also chalk full of child raping, and torture. Oh but the Opium was liberated so at least the CIA has a vast black ops budget from the narco-trade.

Building a wall on the US's southern border isn't going to stop the CIA from flying right over it with their drugs and their guns as they have been doing for 6 decades and counting.

But hey don't you want to raise taxes on the rich and give our benevolent government even more money? The state doesn't care about you, at all. [148]

CHAPTER 25

Fighting Back

"Most Propaganda is not designed to fool the critical thinker but only to give moral cowards the excuse not to think at all."

– Michael Rivero

Defeating the corporate conglomerate's psychological war against the public means keeping a free and open Internet. From the next presidential election cycle onward, victory will become more and more dependent on the dissemination of news online, which is not filtered the way that televised news is today. Each election, the number of people voting third-party is growing. The number of new ideas continues to grow as well. That you have this book is proof of that. The politicians are turning the heat up on the frogs because they know the writing is on the wall. Their days of rule are numbered. The Fed's days of usury and rule from the shadows are numbered as well.

One thing that is not helping our cause is what I call "fear monger alternative media". These outfits love to throw around words like "elite", which automatically grants government parasites a superior image. There are no elites, though; there are simply criminals. Anyone can get rich through theft. There is nothing intellectual or complex about counterfeiting money. But this new, fear-mongering media likes to portray plutocrats as the untouchable rulers of everything (who will someday round you up like cattle and put you in FEMA camps, or release a super-virus that will kill half the planet).139

This kind of attitude is psychologically crippling. They keep their narrative intentionally vague, too, never giving you many names or documentation. Instead they toss around important-sounding terms like

"New World Order", 140 "globalists", and sometimes even more ridiculous things like "Luciferians" or "Illuminati". These kinds of generic paths to nowhere serve as little more than conspiratainment. Recent incarnations have been "the elite" or "the deep state" with no real relationship as to who or what this is other than vaguely governments. Fear sells, but that is not the emotion patriots should be using to galvanize a movement. What we need is will.

The government is, by and large, a bunch of frail, weak old men, the majority of which are not very well-educated or possess any special skills. Most congressmen do not read the bills they support because they would not understand them.141 They rely heavily on twenty-something-year old legislative assistants just to manage their own offices. They have no idea how to manage a nation and have become nothing more than dysfunctional yes-men to the lobbies.

We can beat these people. The only advantage they have is the mass media, which controls the elections. It propagates authoritarianism and fear to keep the system together. If we place all our eggs in one basket, let it be in building a true, independent media, free of sensationalism and fear mongering.

Going forward, our goals should be to end the Federal Reserve System, withdraw from all wars and occupations (direct or by proxy), cut our enormous government waste, and uphold the Constitution. We have no need for three-letter institutions like the DHS TSA, NSA, BIS or MIC.

Step one in winning the psych war is the creation of a new media. It will not take as much money as it may seem. We don't even need a fraction of the cost compared to those we are up against because it's far more expensive to produce a lie than tell the truth. The truth is on our side and it will prevail if it has a chance to be heard.

This is why protecting the internet from censorship is absolutely vital in our struggle for justice. Support good web-based journalism. In these early days, the men and women producing podcasts and publishing blogs are supported through donations or work for free. We are only in the infancy of the online press, but if we support it, it could become the mainstream media of the future.

Blockchain technology to decentralize media platforms is key. On March 4th 2018 my YouTube was terminated and 12 years worth of political videos were removed. This is why it is crucial to back up all your data and place things on the web with redundancy. They can not stop it and the blatant attempts at censorship show their fear. On April 23rd my account was restored after many appeals. But for how long? It already has had videos removed and strikes given for speaking out against Israel's apartheid. Fascism and intolerance has come under the guise of fighting fascism and intolerance. Hate Speech laws fortify support by claiming that they are only for censoring calls to violence, humiliation or prejudice. And yet that simply isn't the case. Hate speech is simply whatever am interest group doesn't like.

Telling the truth and defending justice might not always get you the most friends, but it will get you the right ones. Social and intellectual revolutions must predicate political revolution for anything worthwhile to last. We really can't curb government corruption until we fix journalism first. Social media platforms are already kowtowing to crybully pressure groups. This will have an unwanted right wing backlash. We have to keep fighting, be it in the

trenches of a great meme war, or writing books about how bad
government solutions usually are.

About the Author

Ryan Dawson is a Cape Hatteras native from the town of Buxton, North Carolina. He is a graduate from the College of William & Mary. Currently living In Osaka, Japan, Mr. Dawson is the author of Welcome to the USSA and a co-author of Why Peace. Mr. Dawson has worked as a geopolitical analyst and political radio host for the former FBI translator, Sibel Edmonds, of Boiling Frogs Post. He's made a variety of political documentaries dealing with a wide range of subjects such as the second Iraq War, the September 11th terrorist attacks, the anthrax affair, covert operations of the CIA, and the JFK assassination.

Mr. Dawson's work has been featured on a variety of television news networks such as Russia Today and MSNBC, as well as on political satire comedy shows like the Daily Show with Jon Stewart. He is regularly interviewed on a number of political radio shows and websites. He currently runs the ANC Report, an independent media outlet with a focus on economic and political news.

Thought Provoking Quotes

"The Right's view of big government and the Left's view of big business are both correct. "-Robert Anton Wilson

"To learn who rules over you, simply find out who you are not allowed to criticize.—Voltaire"

"In a time of universal deceit - telling the truth is a revolutionary act" - George Orwell

"Our country's founders cherished liberty, not democracy."- Dr. Ron Paul

"Money is power, and in that government which pays all the public officers of the states will all political power be substantially concentrated" -President Andrew Jackson

"Seldom is the question asked, "_Is_ our children learning?" - President George W. Bush

"I've now been in fifty seven states? I think one left to go. One left to go. Alaska and Hawaii, I was not allowed to go to even though I really wanted to visit but my staff would not justify it." -President Barack Obama

"I once said to my father, when I was a boy, 'Dad we need a third political party.' He said to me, 'I'll settle for a second.'" –Ralph Nader

"Progress is impossible without change, and those who cannot change their minds cannot change anything."- George Bernard Shaw

"Unthinking respect for authority is the greatest enemy of truth." –Albert Einstein

"A government that robs Peter to pay Paul can always depend on the support of Paul."- George Bernard Shaw

"1913 wasn't a very good year. 1913 gave us the income tax, the 16th amendment and the IRS."- Dr. Ron Paul

"It takes time to persuade men to do even what is for their own good." – President Thomas Jefferson.

"It is the mark of an educated mind to be able to entertain a thought without accepting it"-Aristotle

"Government is not reason; it is not eloquent; it is force. Like fire, it is a dangerous servant and a fearful master."-President George Washington

"Any excuse will serve a tyrant" –Aesop

"War does not determine who is right, only who is left." -Bertrand Russell

"Tyranny is the deliberate removal of nuance" – Albert Maysles

"Of all tyrannies, a tyranny exercised 'for the good of its victims' may be the most oppressive." -C.S. Lewis

"We Americans have no commission from God to police the world." – Benjamin Franklin

"Those who make peaceful revolution impossible will make violent revolution inevitable." John F. Kennedy

"Let's dress up like vaginas and parade down the street because, in a covertly recorded private conversation, Donald Trump was rude. What Obama bombed 7 countries and murdered tens of thousands of women? Yes, yes, but did he use rude language, because that's what's important" –Ryan Dawson (saying sarcastically)

"Most Propaganda is not designed to fool the critical thinker but only to give moral cowards the excuse not to think at all." –Mike Rivero

"I have been up to see the Congress and they do not seem to be able to do anything except to eat peanuts and chew tobacco, while my army is starving" _Gen. Robert E. Lee

"It is better to debate a question without settling it than to settle a question without debating it." - Joseph Joubert

"When Liberals don't have a witch to hunt they will just make one up with all the same vigor. After all it's never been about justice, rather about feeling morally superior to others." –Dawson

"Conservatism is not about tradition and morality, hasn't been for many decades… It is about the putative biological and spiritual superiority of the wealthy." –Greg Bear

"Much of the social history of the western world, over the past three decades, has been a system of replacing what worked with what sounded good."- Thomas Sowell

 "It is the consumers who make poor people rich and rich people poor." - Ludwig von Mises

"I was really too honest a man to be a politician and live." -Socrates

"Every election is a sort of advance auction sale of stolen goods." H. L. Mencken

"If you want watch a simple project become something complex and expensive, just task the government with doing it."

"I'm like a chimpanzee, in a tree, jumping up and down, warning other chimpanzees when I see a big cat coming through the woods... I'm the weirdo? Because I'm sitting in a tree going OOH OOH AAH AAH AAH OOH AAH AAH OOH OOH OOH AAH AAH AAH AAH AAH!?" Alex Jones

END NOTES

[1] DiLorenzo, Thomas J., "The Friedmanite Corruption of Capitalism." Ludwig von Mises Institute. http://mises.org/daily/6439/The-Friedmanite-Corruption- of-Capitalism (Accessed January 19, 2014).

[2] Mullins, Eustace. The Secrets of the Federal Reserve.
Bridger House Publishers, 2009.

[3] Still, Bill. Jekyll Island. DVD. Directed by Bill Still. Sun
Valley: Brighter Day Productions, 2013.

[4] A clever method of pooling together cash flow- generating assets of variable risk and bundling them into discrete packages that can be sold to investors. These pooled assets serve as collateral for the CDO. See also "Collaterized Debt Obligations (CDO) Definition". Investopedia.com.

http://www.investopedia.com/terms/c/cdo.asp. (accessed February 12, 2014).

[5] The use of borrowed capital (debt) to increase the potential return of an investment. Leverage increases as the debt-to-equity ratio increases. See also "Leverage Definition". Investopedia.com.
http://www.investopedia.com/terms/l/leverage.asp (accessed February 12, 2014).

[6] An SIV is a pool of investment assets created to attempt to realize profit from credit spreads between short-term debt and long-term structured finance products such asasset-backed securities (ABS). See also "Structured Investment Vehicle (SIV) Definition". Investopedia.com. http://www.investopedia.com/terms/s/structured-investment- vehicle.asp (accessed January 22nd, 2014).

[7] A special loan system for financial institutions offered by the Federal Reserve. It involves offering secured loans to banks, intended to stabilize markets by ensuring that the banks stay liquid. See also "Discount Window Definition". Investopedia.com. http://www.investopedia.com/terms/d/discountwindow.asp (accessed February 24, 2014).

[8] Greenstein, Tracy. "The Fed's $16 Trillion Bailouts Under- Reported". Forbes. September 20, 2011.
http://www.forbes.com/sites/traceygreenstein/2011/09/20/the- feds-16-trillion-bailouts-under-reported/ (accessed February 24
2014).

[9] Dawson, Ryan. "Geopolitics with Ryan Dawson – End the Biggest Financial Scam in History". Boiling Frogs Post. March 4, 2013.

http://www.boilingfrogspost.com/2013/03/04/geopolitics-with- ryan-dawson-end-the-biggest-financial-scam-in-history/ (accessed February 24, 2014).

[10] Webster, Steven C. "United States Government Accountability Office: Report to Congressional Addressees". July 2011. http://ja.scribd.com/doc/60553686/GAO-Fed-Investigation (accessed January 22, 2014).

[11] Napolitano, Andrew P. Lies the Government Told You.
Nashville: Thomas Nelson, 2012.

[12] Ratigan, Dylan. Greedy Bastards: How We Can Stop Corporate Communists, Banksters, and Other Vampires from Sucking America Dry. New York: Simon & Schuster, 2012.
[13] Ben Swann's site can be found at http://benswann.com/
(accessed January 22, 2014)

[14] Matthews, Merrill. "Never Let A Good 'Scandal' Go To Waste, As Conservatives Push Their Agenda". Forbes. May 16, 2013.
http://www.forbes.com/sites/merrillmatthews/2013/05/16/never
-let-a-good-scandal-go-to-waste-as-conservatives-push-their-
agenda/ (accessed February 24, 2014).

[15] Weisenthal, Joel. "RIP: The Bush Tax Cuts". Business Insider. January 2, 2013.
http://www.businessinsider.com/rip-the-bush-tax-cuts-they-have-become-the-
obama-tax-cuts-2013-1

[16] Nolan, Hamilton. "The Unfairness and Stupidity of the Payroll Tax". Gawker.
February 22, 2013. http://gawker.com/5986230/the-unfairness-and-stupidity-of-
the-payroll-tax

[17] Krauthammer, Charles. "Et tu, Jack Lew?" The Washington Post. March 11, 2011.
http://www.washingtonpost.com/wp-
dyn/content/article/2011/03/10/AR2011031005932.html

[18] Miller, Mark. "Five things you should know about Social Security". The Washington Post. August 30, 2013. http://www.reuters.com/article/2013/08/30/us-
column-miller- security-idUSBRE97T0OQ20130830

[19] Campaign at http://www.occupystudentdebtcampaign.org

[20] Lindorff, Dave. "Holding Transcripts Hostage". Los Angeles Times. May 2, 2012. http://articles.latimes.com/2012/may/02/opinion/la-oe-lindorff- student-loan-default-20120502

[21] "Protecting Bad Teachers". Teachers Union Exposed. http://teachersunionexposed.com/protecting.php

[22] Mooney, John. "The List: Which NJ School Districts Spend The Most Money per Student?" NJ Spotlight. October 21, 2013. http://www.njspotlight.com/stories/13/10/20/the-list-which-nj- school-districts-spend-the-most-money-per-student/

[23] Sykes, Christopher. The Best Mind Since Einstein. VHS. BBC-TV (Horizon) 1993. http://www.youtube.com/watch?v=_ah7f-1M2Sg

[24] https://www.forbes.com/sites/realspin/2016/09/19/the-discrimination-in-college-admissions-nobody-is-talking-about/#67d88781658c

[25] Bowdon, Bob. The Cartel. DVD/Blu-ray. 2009.

[26] Leutwyler, Kristin. "Most U.S. Antibiotics Fed to Healthy Livestock". Scientific American. Jan 10, 2001. http://www.scientificamerican.com/article/most-us-antibiotics- fed-t/

[27] Oppel, Richard A., Jr. "Taping of Farm Cruelty Is Becoming the Crime". The New York Times. April 6, cruelty-is-becoming-the-crime.html

[28] Perry, Mark J. "California Puts Raw Dairy Farmers in Jail; While in France, Raw Milk is Sold in Vending Machines". Carpe Diem: Professor Mark J. Perry's Blog for Economics and Finance. August 20, 2012. http://mjperry.blogspot.jp/2012/08/california-puts-raw-dairy- farmers-in.html

[29] Lockheed Martin: Science, Research, & Development. http://www.lockheedmartinjobs.com/science-research- dev.asp

[30] "Monsanto official Beaten by farmers in India over Failed GMO Bt Cotton Seeds". Salem-News.com. July 12, 2011. http://www.salem-news.com/articles/july122011/india-monsanto-beaten-tk.php

[31] For more information, visit "Energy from Thorium" at

http://energyfromthorium.com

[32] "004-027". Presidential Recordings Program. June 4, 1971. http://whitehousetapes.net/transcript/nixon/004-027

[33] Sorenson, Kirk. "Thorium, an Alternative Nuclear Fuel". TEDx, April 2011. http://www.ted.com/talks/kirk_sorensen_thorium_an_alternativ e_nuclear_fuel.html

[34] Chan, Norman. "Why the F.A.A. Has Been Slow to Approve Electronic Devices on Airplanes". Tested. March 21, 2012. http://www.tested.com/tech/43465-why-the-faa-has-been-slow-to-approve-electronic-devices-on-airplanes/

[35] McClellan, J. Mac. "How Certification Rules Are Hurting Us". Left Seat. December 6, 2012. http://macsblog.com/2012/12/how-certification-rules-are- hurting-us/

[36] "TSA Misses Guns, Bombs In Tests". Judicial Watch. December 20, 2010. http://www.judicialwatch.org/blog/2010/12/tsa-misses-guns-bombs-tests/

[37] Marshall, Jonathan. Peter Dale Scott, Jane Hunter. The Iran-Contra Connection: Secret Teams and Covert Operations in Reagan Era. Cambridge: South End Press, 1987

[38] The illegal practice of short-selling shares that may not actually exist. See also "Naked Shorting Definition". Investopedia.com. http://www.investopedia.com/terms/n/nakedshorting.asp

[39] The ratio of the trading volume of put options to call options, used as an indicator of investor optimism about the market. See also "Put-Call Definition", Investopedia.com. http://www.investopedia.com/terms/p/putcallratio.asp

[40] Wald, Matthew L. "F.A.A. Official Scrapped Tape of 6, 2004. http://www.nytimes.com/2004/05/06/national/06CND- TAPE.html
[41] "Is Military Research Hazardous to Veterans' Health? Lessons Spanning Half a Century". Gulfwarvets.com. http://www.gulfwarvets.com/senate.htm

[42] Bazell, Robert. "U.S. Apologizes for Guatemala STD Experiments". NBC News.com. October 1, 2010. http://www.nbcnews.com/id/39456324/ns/health-

sexual_health/t/us-apologizes-guatemala-std- experiments/#.UwsFhnl5Phs

[43] Rothbard, Murray. "Origins Of Progressive Regulation".
http://www.youtube.com/watch?v=62rl8OYFzGg

[44] Robert B. Anderson, 76, Pleads Guilty to Tax Evasion, Bank Fraud". LA Times.
March 27, 1987. http://articles.latimes.com/1987-03-27/business/fi-127_1_tax-
evasion

[45] Why Can't Chuck Get His Business off the Ground?
Institute for Justice. http://www.ij.org/freedomflix/37- citystudiesvideo

[46] Dawson, Ryan. How They Bleep You. YouTube. March
15, 2009. https://www.youtube.com/watch?v=mZ55zegkV6Q

[47] "Ron Paul: Foreign Aid Takes Money From Poor In U.S., Given To Rich Tax Evasion,
Bank Fraud". Real Clear Politics. October 18.2011.
http://www.realclearpolitics.com/video/2011/10/18/ron_paul_f
oreign_aid_takes_money_from_poor_in_us_given_to_rich.htm

[48] Glaser, John. "Uzbek Dictator Shifts From Boiling
People to Freezing Them". Antiwar.Blog. November 4,
2011. http://antiwar.com/blog/2011/11/04/uzbek-dictator- shifts-from-boiling-
people-to-freezing-them/

[49] Mountain, Thomas C. "Carnage in the Congo". Counter Punch. December , 2012.
http://www.counterpunch.org/2012/12/24/carnage-in-the- congo/

[50] "The Pain of Suspension". The Economist. January 12,
2013. http://www.economist.com/news/middle-east-and- africa/21569438-will-
rwandas-widely-praised-development- plans-now-be-stymied-pain

[51] "Bill Text Versions 110th Congress (2007-2008)". The Library of Congress: Thomas.
http://thomas.loc.gov/cgi- bin/query/z?c110:S.2191:/

[52] Dawson, Ryan. "Geopolitics with Ryan Dawson- Episode 2: The Shuffling of the
Generals". Boiling Frog Post. November 19, 2012.
http://www.boilingfrogspost.com/2012/11/19/geopolitics-with- ryan-dawson-
episode-2-the-shuffling-of-the-generals/

[53] "Findings from a CDC Report on the 1946-1948 U.S.
Public Health Service Sexually Transmitted Disease (STD) Inoculation Study".

HHS.gov - US Department of Health and Human Services. September 30, 2010.
http://www.hhs.gov/1946inoculationstudy/findings.html
[54] For a look at what happened after the delicate balance of the ecosystem was restored, check out the short film, How Wolves Change Rivers.
http://www.youtube.com/watch?v=ysa5OBhXz-Q

[55] Trogdon, Jim. "Guest Column: Correcting Some Errors in Statements by SELC on Bonner Bridge". Island Free Press. December 10, 2013.
http://www.islandfreepress.org/2013Archives/12.10.2013-GuestColumnCorrectingSomeErrorsInStatementsBySELCOnBonnerBridge.html

[56] Ahmed, Nafeez. "How The World Health Organisation Covered Up Iraq's Nuclear Nightmare". The Guardian. October 13, 2013.
http://www.theguardian.com/environment/earth- insight/2013/oct/13/world-health-organisation-iraq-war- depleted-uranium

[57] Rasor, Dina. "DuPont C8 Lawsuit | DuPont C8 Class Action Lawsuit". Wright & Schulte, LLC. May 17, 2012. http://yourlegalhelp.com/dupont-c8-lawsuit-dupont-c8-class- action-lawsuit

[58] "DuPont Hid Teflon Pollution For Decades".
Environmental Working Group. December 13, 2002.
http://www.ewg.org/research/dupont-hid-teflon-pollution- decades

[59] Michael Jackson - They Don't Care About Us (Brazil Version) (Official Video)
https://www.youtube.com/watch?v=QNJL6nfu_Q

[60] Sandholm, Drew. Tom Rotunno. "U.S. Postal Service Alcohol Delivery Idea Criticized By Merchants". The Huffington Post. August 11, 2013.
http://www.huffingtonpost.com/2013/08/11/postal-service- alcohol-delivery-idea_n_3740349.html

[61] Plumer, Brad. "The Post Office is Defying Congress by Halting Saturday Mail. But why?". The Washington Post
http://www.washingtonpost.com/blogs/wonkblog/wp/2013/02/06/the-post-office-is-defying-congress-by-halting-saturday-deliveries-why/

[62] The U.S. Postal Service". Environmental Working Group. September 21, 2011.
http://mrzine.monthlyreview.org/2011/nader230911.html

[63] Lichtenstein, Jesse. "Do We Really Want to Live Without the Post Office?".
Esquire. February 2013. http://www.esquire.com/print-this/post-office-business-

<u>trouble-</u>
0213

[64] "10 Highest-Paid Government Jobs - 2. Postmaster General: Patrick R. Donahue". Comcast.net. <u>http://xfinity.comcast.net/slideshow/finance-</u> <u>highpaidgovtjobs/postmaster-general/</u>

[65] Page 72 United States Postal Regulatory Commission 10-K
https://www.prc.gov/docs/97/97841/2016-11-15%20USPS%2010-K.pdf

[66] Bill Conroy on the CIA moving Cocaine http://www.ancreport.com/podcast/bill-conroy/
[67] Jeremy R. Hammond, Jeremy R. Hammond. "Crashed Jet Carrying Cocaine Linked to CIA". Dissident Voice. September 13th, <u>2008.</u> <u>http://dissidentvoice.org/2008/09/crashed-jet-carrying-cocaine- linked-to-cia/</u>

[68] Serrano, Richard A. Serrano. "Fast and Furious Weapons Were Found in Mexico Cartel Enforcer's Home". Los Angeles Times. October 8, 2011. <u>http://www.latimes.com/news/nationworld/nation/la-na-atf- guns-</u> <u>20111009,0,6431788.story#axzz2tNM1GW5Y</u>

[69] "US Govt Struck Deal With Mexican Drug Cartel In Exchange For Info - Report". RT USA. January 14, 2014
[70] Kelly, Michael. "CONFIRMED: The DEA Struck A Deal With Mexico's Most Notorious Drug Cartel". Business Insider. January 13, 2014. <u>http://www.businessinsider.com/the-us-government-and-the- sinaloa-cartel-2014-1</u>

[71] Secret Detention and Extraordinary Rendition". Open Society Foundations. February 2013. <u>http://www.opensocietyfoundations.org/reports/globalizing-</u> <u>torture-cia-secret-detention-and-extraordinary-rendition</u>

[72] Dawson, Ryan. "Bill Conroy on Cocaine Planes from the CIA". ANC Report. February 12, 2014. <u>http://ancreport.com/podcasts/podcast.php?id=88</u>

[73] "CIA Plane Crash Lands with Four Tons of Coke".
Independent Canadian News. April 14, 2011.
<u>http://arnpriornews.wordpress.com/2011/04/14/cia-plane- crash-land-with-four-</u> <u>tons-of-coke/</u>

[74] Dawson, Ryan. "Doug Valetine on the CIA and the Phony War on Drugs". ANC Report. February 09, 2014. <u>http://ancreport.com/podcasts/podcast.php?id=87</u>

75 "Guns are Illegal in Mexico". Consulate General of the United States | Tijuana, Mexico. February 15, 2014. http://tijuana.usconsulate.gov/tijuana/warning.html

76 "After Mexican resort shootout". Fox News.com. January 02, 2014. http://www.foxnews.com/world/2014/01/02/gun- from-botched-fast-and-furious-operation-turns-up-after- mexican-resort/

77 Book, Doug. "Eric Holder's Two Decades of Concealing Murder". The Western School for Journalism. July 7, 2012. http://www.westernjournalism.com/eric-holders-two- decades-of-concealing-murder/

78 Craddock, Corinna. "San Diego - New Developments in Police Shooting Case of Aiyana Stanley Jones". Examiner.com. March 15, 2011. http://www.examiner.com/article/san-diego-new- U

79 Valencia, Nick, Adriana Hauser. "Family Wants Answers in Florida Teen's Death after Tasering". CNN. August 9, 2013. http://edition.cnn.com/2013/08/08/us/florida- taser-death/

80 Dawson, Ryan. "Will Grigg on Out-of-control Police". ANC Report. November 14, 2013. http://ancreport.com/podcasts/podcast.php?id=55

81 Quigley, Rachel. "Caught on Tape: Police Beat and Taser 'Gentle' Mentally-Ill Homeless Man To Death". Mail Online. July 29, 2011. http://www.dailymail.co.uk/news/article-2019225/Kelly- Thomas-Police-beat-taser-gentle-mentally-ill-homeless-man- death.html

82 For more from Will Grigg, check out his site, Pro Libertate, at http://freedominourtime.blogspot.jp

83 Croatoan Archaeological Society. http://www.cashatteras.com/

84 Dawson, Ryan. Lost Colony Play vs Lost Colony History. Youtube. June 22, 2011. http://www.youtube.com/watch?v=SqfXUGg0Y0l

85 Colavito, Jason. "Review of America Unearthed S01E07: 'Mystery of Roanoke'". JasonColavito.com. February 2, 2013.

http://www.jasoncolavito.com/1/post/2013/02/review-of- america-unearthed-s01e07-mystery-of-roanoke.html

86 "Operation WASHTUB - CIA, Russia, Nicaragua, Guatemala 1954". Laboratory of Hidden Alternatives. July 2, 2012. http://laboratoryofhiddenalternatives.wordpress.com/2012/07/02/operation-washtub-cia-russia-nicaragua-guatemala-1954/

87 Schwartz, Stephen. The Two Faces of Islam: The House of Sa'ud from Tradition to Terror. Garden City: Doubleday, 2002.

88 Marquis, Christopher. "Enron's Many Strands: The Army Secretary; The Pentagon Opens Inquiry on Travels in Military Jet". The New York Times. March 29, 2002. http://www.nytimes.com/2002/03/29/business/enron-s-many- strands-army-secretary-pentagon-opens-inquiry-travels-military-jet.html

89 "USS Fort Worth Comes to Life". Lockheed Martin. September 22, 2012. http://www.lockheedmartin.com/us/mst/features/120922-uss- fort-worth-comes-to-life.html

90 Jackson, David. "Hersh Uncovered Pentagon Adviser Richard Perle's Role in Securing Homeland Security Contracts". Chicago Tribune. June 25, 2004. http://www.chicagotribune.com/features/chi- hershbar2,0,2912239.story

91 Kay, Joseph. "Bush Administration Embroiled in Boeing Scandal". World Socialist Web Site. December 17, 2003. http://www.wsws.org/en/articles/2003/12/boeg-d17.html

92 Jackson, David. "This Day in History: Seymour Hersh breaks My Lai Story". History.com. Nov 12, 1969. http://www.history.com/this-day-in-history/seymour-hersh- breaks-my-lai-story

93 Hersh, Seymour M. "Torture at Abu Ghraib". The New Yorker. May 10, 2004. http://www.newyorker.com/archive/2004/05/10/040510fa_fact

94 Burton, James. The Pentagon Wars Directed by Richard Benjamin. HBO, 1998

95 Austin, Mark. "The Bradley Fighting Vehicle". A. James Clark School of Engineering. September 23, 2010.

http://www.eng.umd.edu/~austin/enes489p/lecture-resources/BradleyFightingVehicle-Scenario.pdf

96 Burton, James. The Pentagon Wars: Reformers Challenge the Old Guard. Annapolis: Naval Institute Press, 1993.

97 "Top 30 Defense Contractors of 2012". Professional Overseas Contractors. December 26, 2012. http://www.your-poc.com/top-30-defense-contractors-of-2012/

98 Wise, Jacob and Brandon Young. "Helicopters, the Tactical Innovation of the Vietnam War". University of Wisconsin - Eau Claire. 2010. http://www.uwec.edu/webprojects/geog445/helicrash_byyeear. html

99 "V22 Osprey Crash". Youtube. July 8, 2007. http://www.youtube.com/watch?v=VYeLishJ_Js

100 Corr, O. Casey. "Prototype Of Boeing's Osprey Explodes, Crashes". The Seattle Times. July 20, 1992. http://community.seattletimes.nwsource.com/archive/?date=19 920720&slug=1503082

101 Hill, Brandon. "Bell-Boeing V-22 Osprey Still Facing Problems". Daily Tech. January 22, 2007. http://www.dailytech.com/BellBoeing+V22+Osprey+Still+Facing+Problems/article5 809.htm

102 Associated Press. "5 Injured in Bell Boeing Osprey Crash in Florida". Herald Net. June 14, 2012. http://www.heraldnet.com/article/20120614/NEWS02/1206199 48

103 "US Deploys MV-22 Osprey Aircraft to Japan Base, 'Locals Go Bananas'". Russia Today. Youtube. October 1, 2012. https://www.youtube.com/watch?v=HlE0YtMzNug

104 Rasor, Dina. "Pilots as Lab Rats: The Reprehensible Risk – Taking on the F-22 Raptor". Truthout.org. May 17, 2012. http://truth-out.org/news/item/9195-pilots-as-lab-rats-the-reprehensible-risk-taking-on-the-f-22-raptor

105 On-Board Oxygen Generation Systems https://aerocontent.honeywell.com/aero/common/documents/myaerospacecatalo

g-documents/Defense_Brochures-documents/Life_Support_Systems.pdf

[106] How DOD's $1.5 Trillion F-35 Broke the Air Force
http://www.cnbc.com/id/101883138

[107] Pentagon: Here are all the problems with the F-35
http://www.businessinsider.com/here-are-all-the-problems-with-the-f-35-that-the-pentagon-found-in-a-2014-report-2015-3

[108] Lockheed promises tailhook fix to Navy's F-35C
https://www.military.com/dodbuzz/2013/04/10/lockheed-promises-tailhook-fix-to-navys-f-35c

[109] http://miragec14.blogspot.jp/2013/01/stealth-coating-peeling-off-from-f-35s.html

[110] http://www.news.com.au/technology/online/security/spy-f35s-send-sensitive-norwegian-military-data-back-to-lockheed-martin-in-the-united-states/news-story/12b4fafce6b579448cc8416518063d1f

[111] https://www.rt.com/usa/416916-f35-pentagon-operations-report/

[112] http://www.corpwatch.org/article.php?id=14307

[113] http://rightweb.irc-online.org/profile/project_on_transitional_democracies/

[114] https://www.washingtonpost.com/business/economy/in-trumps-budget-lockheed-looms-almost-as-large-as-the-state-department/2018/02/15/e7eb3aa8-11c1-11e8-9570-29c9830535e5_story.html?utm_term=.1060cafd0f88

[115] 911 Research for Grown ups https://www.youtube.com/watch?v=oWjuRQdvn1o

[116] Lockheed Martin Wants to Merge an F-22 and F-35 Into 1 Fighter for Japan. It Won't Happen. http://nationalinterest.org/blog/the-buzz/lockheed-martin-wants-merge-f-22-f-35-1-fighter-japan-it-25509

[117] 117   Yinon, Oded. "A Strategy for Israel in the Nineteen Eighties". Translation by

Irael Shahak, June 13, 1982. Originally appeared in KIVUNIM (Directions), A Journal for Judaism and Zionism. Issue 14. February 1982. http://cosmos.ucc.ie/cs1064/jabowen/IPSC/articles/article0005345.html

[118] Chossudovsky, Michel. "The Spoils of War: Afghanistan's Multibillion Dollar Heroin Trade". Global Research. June 14, 2005. http://www.globalresearch.ca/the-spoils-of-war-afghanistan-s-multibillion-dollar-heroin-trade/91

[119] Dawson, Ryan. "Time to Get Out of Afghanistan". Youtube. Dec 17, 2013. https://www.youtube.com/watch?v=7T9U17WrsX8

[120] Shin, Laura. "The 85 Richest People In The World Have As Much Wealth As The 3.5 Billion Poorest". Forbes. January 23, 2014. http://www.forbes.com/sites/laurashin/2014/01/23/the-85- richest-people-in-the-world-have-as-much-wealth-as-the-3-5- billion-poorest/

[121] Dawson, Ryan. "The Top 20% Have No Idea How The Bottom 40% Get By". Rys2Sense. July 18, 2013. http://www.rys2sense.com/anti-neocons/viewtopic.php?f=114&t=32298

[122] 123 Shine, Tom. "47% of Congress Members Millionaires — a Status Shared by Only 1% of Americans". ABC News. Nov 16, 2011. http://abcnews.go.com/blogs/politics/2011/11/47-of-congress- members-millionaires-a-status-shared-by-only-1-of-americans/

[123] Gilson, Dave. Carolyn Perot. "It's the Inequality, Stupid". Mother Jones. March 2011. http://www.motherjones.com/politics/2011/02/income- inequality-in-america-chart-graph

[124] Horton, Scott. "Scott Horton Interviews john Cusack". Audio. Anti-war Radio. May 22 2008. http://antiwar.com/radio/2008/05/22/john-cusack/

[125] "Wage Statistics for 2011". Social Security Online. February 20, 2014. http://www.ssa.gov/cgi- bin/netcomp.cgi?year=2011

[126] 127 Sowell, Thomas. "The 'Trickle-down' Economics Straw Man". Capitalism Magazine. September 27, 2001. http://capitalismmagazine.com/2001/09/the-trickle-down- economics-straw-man/

127 "Warren Buffet Rides the Bailout Gravy Train". Thom Hartman Program. March 28, 2013. http://www.thomhartmann.com/forum/2013/03/warren-buffet- rides-bailout-gravy-train

128 Piller, Charles. "Buffett, Champion Of Bailout, Is Also Leading Beneficiary". McClatchyDC. April 5, 2009. http://www.mcclatchydc.com/2009/04/05/65496/buffett- champion-of-bailout-is.html

129 131 Stern, Marlow. "'Mission Congo' Alleges Pat Robertson Exploited Post-Genocide Rwandans For Diamonds". The Daily Beast. September 7, 2013. http://www.thedailybeast.com/articles/2013/09/07/doc-mission-congo-alleges-pat-robertson-exploited-post-genocide- rwandans-for-diamonds.html

130 Grobel, Lawrence. "Playboy Interview: Jesse Ventura". Playboy. November, 1999.

131 Mazzetti, Mark, Charlie Savage and Scott Shane. "How a U.S. Citizen Came to Be in America's Cross Hairs". The New York Times. March 9, 2013. http://www.nytimes.com/2013/03/10/world/middleeast/anwar- al-awlaki-a-us-citizen-in-americas-cross-hairs.html?pagewanted=all&_r=1&

132 Friedersdorf, Conor. "How Team Obama Justifies the Killing of a 16-Year-Old American". The Atlantic. October 24, 2012. http://www.theatlantic.com/politics/archive/2012/10/how- team-obama-justifies-the-killing-of-a-16-year-old- american/264028/

133 Wafa, Abdul Waheed and Mark McDonald. "Deadly US Airstrike Said to Hit Afghan Wedding Party." The New York Times. November 5, 2008. http://www.nytimes.com/2008/11/05/world/asia/05iht- afghan.3.17553439.html

134 Greenwald, Glenn. "US Drones Targeting Rescuers and Mourners". Salon. February 5, 2012. http://www.salon.com/2012/02/05/u_s_drones_targeting_rescuers_and_mourners/

135 Hauser, Christine. "The Aftermath of Drone Strikes on a Wedding Convoy in Yemen". The Lede. February 1, 2012. http://thelede.blogs.nytimes.com/2013/12/19/the- aftermath-of-drone-strikes-on-a-wedding-convoy-in-yemen/

136 Jones, Alex. "No More Bullshit: James Cameron Runs From Threat of Bio Attack, Economic Collapse". Youtube. February 1, 2012. https://www.youtube.com/watch?v=_GIfxQc_9d8

137 Dawson, Ryan. "OK, Alex, Settle Down There, Doomsayer". Youtube. February 5, 2012. http://www.youtube.com/watch?v=lpSh349C4mg

138 "Pelosi: 'We Have to Pass the Bill So That You Can Find Out What Is In It'". Youtube. March 9, 2010 http://www.youtube.com/watch?v=hV-05TLiiLU

139 A cleansing fire: Moral outrage alleviates guilt and buffers threats to one's moral identity https://link.springer.com/article/10.1007/s11031-017-9601-2

140 Thomas Sowell on how affirmative action hurts minorities http://www.youtube.com/watch?v=VVvnTByzTmA

141 Thomas Sowell breaks down Welfare's results141 https://www.youtube.com/watch?v=2GklCBvS-el

142 Ronda Rousey shuts down unequal myth https://www.youtube.com/watch?v=ZLrNBmXhr1M

143 League Refuses to "Help Perpetrate a Fraud". League of Women Voters. October 3, 1988. http://www.lwv.org/press- releases/league-refuses-help-perpetrate-fraud

144 Farah, George. No Debate: How the Republican and Democratic Parties Secretly Control the Presidential Debates. New York: Seven Stories Press, 2004.

145 Classified Evidence: US Soldiers Raped Boys In Front Of Their Mothers https://www.mintpressnews.com/classified-evidence-us-soldiers-raped-boys-in-front-of-their-mothers/200160/

146 US general linked to Abu Ghraib abuse http://www.theguardian.com/world/2004/may/22/iraq.usa1

147 Iraqi prisoners 'treated no worse than cheerleaders' https://www.telegraph.co.uk/news/worldnews/northamerica/usa/1480923/Iraqi-prisoners-treated-no-worse-than-cheerleaders.html

[148] George Carlin The American Dream
https://www.youtube.com/watch?v=BK3nmXZp9Ig

www.ingramcontent.com/pod-product-compliance
Lightning Source LLC
Chambersburg PA
CBHW060042260726

48658CB00004B/1159